YOU
WERE MADE FOR
MORE

Other Books by Jim Cymbala

Storm
(book and audio)

Spirit Rising
(book and audio)

Fresh Wind, Fresh Fire
(book and audio)

Fresh Faith
(book and audio)

Fresh Power
(book and audio)

The Life God Blesses
(book and audio)

The Church God Blesses
(book and audio)

Breakthrough Prayer
(book and audio)

When God's People Pray
(curriculum)

THE LIFE YOU HAVE
THE LIFE GOD WANTS YOU TO HAVE

YOU
WERE MADE FOR
MORE

JIM CYMBALA
with DEAN MERRILL

Z ZONDERVAN®

ZONDERVAN

You Were Made for More
Copyright © 2008 Jim Cymbala

This title is also available in a Zondervan audio edition.
Visit www.zondervan.com/fm.

Requests for information should be addressed to:
Zondervan, 3900 *Sparks Dr. SE*, Grand Rapids, Michigan 49546

This edition: ISBN 978-0-310-34088-1 (softcover)

Library of Congress Cataloging-in-Publication Data

Cymbala, Jim, 1943–
        You were made for more : the life you have, the life God wants you to have /
    Jim Cymbala, Dean Merrill.
            p.   cm.
        ISBN 978-0-310-24127-0 (hardcover, jacketed)
        1. Spirituality—Biblical teaching. 2. Christian life. I. Merrill, Dean. II. Title.
    BS680.S7C96   2008
    248.4—dc22   2008016706

All Scripture quotations, unless otherwise indicated, are taken from the *Holy Bible,
Today's New International Version* ™. TNIV®. Copyright © 2002, 2004 by Biblica, Inc.®
Used by permission. All rights reserved worldwide. Some quotations include italics for
emphasis that does not appear in the original text.

Scripture quotations marked NKJV are from *The New King James Bible Version.*
Copyright © 1979, 1980, 1982, Thomas Nelson, Inc.

Scriptures quotations marked NASB are from the *New American Standard Bible.*
Copyright © 1960, 1962, 1963, 1968, 1971, 1972, 1973, 1975, 1977, 1995 by The Lockman
Foundation. Used by permission.

Internet addresses (websites, blogs, etc.) and telephone numbers in this book are
offered as a resource to you. These are not intended in any way to be or imply an
endorsement on the part of Zondervan, nor do we vouch for the content of these sites
and numbers for the life of this book.

Published in association with the literary agency of Ann Spangler and Company, 1420
Pontiac Road S.E., Grand Rapids, MI 49506.

Interior design: Beth Shagene

First printing November 2014

CONTENTS

CONTENTS

CHAPTER 1

STEP UP

If you come to visit us here in New York City, you will have a wonderful time—as long as you avoid one thing. You can go shopping along Fifth Avenue, take in a Broadway play, climb the Statue of Liberty, see a Mets or Yankees baseball game, do the tour at the New York Stock Exchange, go up to the top of the Empire State Building, take a carriage ride through Central Park—and of course be sure to come see us at the Brooklyn Tabernacle for one of our three Sunday services or the Tuesday night prayer meeting. Just don't look at our housing costs.

Two-bedroom condos and co-ops in nice areas of Manhattan usually start around $2,000,000. Then, of course, you will pay an extra $700 a month or more for "common charges" in the building: trash removal, the doorman at the front, maintenance of the entryway, the elevator, etc. If you would rather just rent, a normal one-bedroom apartment goes for $3,000 a month; a small "studio" apartment (where your bed is part of your living area) rents in the $2,000 range.

One young woman in our church told me she was living in two tiny rooms in a building that was "falling apart," where she had a bathtub in the kitchen, but the toilet was down the hall—and she was paying $800 a month in rent. That was a bargain, thanks to what New Yorkers know as *rent stabilization.* This is a complicated city regulation that tries to hold the lid on costs. "But as soon as I move out," she added, "they're going to do a bit of remodeling—replace the tub with a small shower, do some plastering. Then for a new lease they can jack it up to $1,800 a month!"

Here at the other end of the Brooklyn Bridge where our church is, a new condominium building is going up around the corner. The smallest studio unit will sell for $1,500,000. And you probably wouldn't call this a "good neighborhood." Your sleep would be punctuated by sirens in the night. There is no place to park your car for less than $250 a month. As many as 5,000 people will reside in the confines of one city *block.*

So what are the alternatives? Every week in our church I meet people who are wishing and yearning for something more spacious that's still affordable. A newly married couple wants to start a family—but where would they even put a crib? Should they pull up stakes and move to the Long Island suburbs? At least they'd have some breathing room, maybe even a little grass out front. But things aren't cheap there, either.

Take Levittown as one example—which is remembered as the first mass-produced suburb in America. Right after World War II, developer Abraham Levitt and his two sons created something called the "ranch" design—for just $7,990. (But you did get a General Electric stove and refrigerator for that price, plus the latest Bendix washing machine!) Block upon block of these modest houses went up, drawing national attention. Critics scorned them as "ticky-tacky" and "cookie cutter." Sales to returning GIs and their growing families, nevertheless, were brisk.

Well ... today a two- or three-bedroom single-family home in Levittown starts at $350,000 and goes up past half a million. And you're not even next to the water. If you work in Manhattan, your commute on the Long Island Rail Road will chew up forty-five minutes each way, plus whatever time you will then spend getting from Penn Station to your workplace. (Assuming the trains are running on time, that is.) If you would rather drive your car to the city, don't even think about it; the Long Island Expressway is known as the world's largest parking lot.

> The desire for a place to breathe, to grow, to be safe runs deep within us all. We want to spread our wings.

The desire for a place to breathe, to grow, to be safe runs deep within us all, of whatever century. And not just in the physical realm. Emotionally and spiritually as well, we hate being cramped. We want to spread our wings. We want to stretch out. Didn't Jesus say, "I have come that they may have life, and *have it to the full*" (John 10:10)? That is what we crave. We sense somehow that we were made for more—more than the constricted, self-limiting lives we currently endure.

Wouldn't it be wonderful, for example, if we could have victory over some of the negative habits and sins that tie us down?

Wouldn't it be great if we were emotionally and spiritually free to find a place to serve God, a ministry of some kind that would let us make a difference in other people's lives?

What if our relationships with our family members—and others, too—were healthy and loving instead of caustic and full of conflict?

What if we learned to pray more often—and actually saw answers to our prayers?

Wouldn't it be wonderful to live each day with a spirit of confidence instead of anxiety and fear?

Here are just a few examples of the "more" that awaits the children of God: A deeper understanding of his Word ... insight into his unique plan for our lives ... an abiding joy in the face of life's setbacks ... power and courage to witness for Christ ... freedom from all the psychological and emotional issues that hold us back ... peace on the inside regardless of external circumstances. The abundant life that God plans for his own children includes all of these.

Stop right now and consider these questions: Do you have similar yearnings for a spiritual life that is fuller and richer in every way? If God brought you into the spiritual counterpart of "a good and spacious land, a land flowing with milk and honey" (Exod. 3:8), what would that look like?

The theme of this book is realizing the fullness of what God has for each one of us as his followers. His Word is packed with exciting promises of blessing. He means to do good for us, not evil. His plans for us are greater than we can ever imagine. The only question is how we get from here to there. What does it take for us to cross the Jordan River to enter into our land flowing with milk and honey—his chosen future for us?

God will make the way. The Brooklyn Tabernacle Choir once recorded an up-tempo Percy Gray song entitled "Keep on Making a Way." It is addressed to God, thanking him for his willingness to take us further and higher than we've ever gone. The chorus says:

> Keep on making a way for me,
> Opening doors for me,
> Taking care of me....
> I will ever sing your praise,

Glory to your name,
Keep on making a way for me.[1]

On the Move

The Bible account of Joshua taking the people of Israel across the Jordan has much to teach us about the way we get into our Promised Land. So do the two Old Testament books that immediately follow: Judges and Ruth. Together, this trio of books shows God's people stepping up to the "more" they had wanted so earnestly back in the desert. God's provision for them is an illustration of his provision for us today.

Be aware that the conquest of the Promised Land—known as Canaan—was not a walk in the park, however. Realizing God's promises did not come easy for the Israelites. Yes, some of the old gospel songs and spirituals speak about heaven in terms of "Canaan's fair and happy land" and "sweet Beulah land." Well, guess what? The Israelites arrived not in heaven, but in enemy territory! To claim the land God had promised them meant facing and defeating all kinds of hostile forces. Canaanite armies were entrenched in the very land Israel had been told would be theirs.

> The conquest of Canaan was not a walk in the park. The Israelites arrived not in heaven, but in enemy territory.

Sometimes they won battles in spectacular fashion; at other times they made serious mistakes that set them back. God had to straighten them out more than once. As the Irish author and Bible teacher J. B. Stoney said back in the 1800s, "It was easier to get Israel *out* of Egypt than to get them *into* Canaan."[2] In other words, even though God had delivered his people from slavery in Egypt, they still struggled to follow his lead into the Promised Land. So it is with us today. If we claim Christ as Savior, we are no longer slaves to sin; yet we still seem to struggle when it comes to claiming God's promise of more. Unfortunately, just like the Israelites, we don't always get it right the first time. We wander off from God's purposes for us, even though they are perfect. He has to urge us on, sometimes forcefully, to do things his way.

These three Bible books teach us as much what *not* to do as what *to* do.

Joshua

Joshua was the handpicked successor to Moses, who had led the Israelites out of Egypt and into the desert, where they journeyed for forty years. The book that bears his name relates how Joshua guided the people across the Jordan River, conquered cities like Jericho and tribes like the Amorites, and settled into the land, which was then divided up among the twelve Israelite tribes.

Some Bible readers cringe at the mere mention of the book of Joshua because of its military violence. It is probably the *bloodiest* book in the Bible. That is because a particularly wicked civilization—known for its idolatry, religious prostitution, sorcery, and even child sacrifice at times—was now coming under divine judgment. Centuries earlier, in the time of Abraham, God was not yet ready to do anything about this wicked civilization; "the sin of the Amorites has not yet reached its full measure," he said (Gen. 15:16). Now, a longsuffering God was finally ready to excise a moral cancer located in Canaan.[3]

Right from the start, God warned his people to remain separate from the Canaanite tribes. He commanded the Israelites not to intermarry or make other alliances. He was

12

saying in essence to his chosen nation, "If you're careless, you will not change *them*; instead, they will change *you*. Your worship of the one true God will get diluted, and then polluted."

Judges

The book of Judges tells about good times and awful times, faithfulness and relapse. The people repeatedly gave in to the very things God had warned against. They began to forget the promise that God had more for them, instead becoming content with what they already had. Because of this, God had to get tough with his own people.

There is actually more gloom than sunshine in Judges, especially near the end. This is perhaps the most *depressing* book in the Bible. It serves to warn us about straying from God's instructions. But we also gain *hope* from seeing a series of courageous leaders—both men and women—whom God raised up whenever the people repented and cried out for his help: Deborah, Gideon, Jephthah, and Samson, to name just a few.

Ruth

In the midst of this same time period, a wonderful cameo shows up: the story of Ruth. She never expected to be anything great. She wasn't even of Israelite descent. And yet God's "more" reached all the way to her, lifting her to an honored place in messianic history. Here is what we might call the most *inspiring* book in the Bible, at least in terms of human drama. It shows God's amazing care for a simple person who cast her allegiance in his direction.

These three books, covering 300 years or so of time, will be our anchor points as we explore how God made us for more. I will also share with you the inspiring stories of people here in our own time who have trusted God to do amazing things in their lives. Vanessa Holland and Bonite Affriany and Kumiko Nakamura and Mark Hill and his wife, Georgina, along with others, will lift your sights and your spirit toward the One for whom nothing is impossible.

Not Just Anywhere

What should we expect in the Promised Land? The future is not of our own choosing, nor is it vague. God has very specific plans in mind. The Promised Land had clear parameters. The Israelites could not just go to Greece or Syria or Arabia and expect that God would give it to them. He wasn't sending them to possess the entire world; he had a definite parcel with definite borders in mind.

Similarly, we cannot go anywhere we like and assume that God will supply the resources of our fantasies. Yes, ours is a spacious and wonderful land. It will be exciting to get there. But it is limited to his specific plan for our lives, and we are assured of God's help if we stay within the boundaries of what he has marked out for us.

I sometimes wonder how many Christians today have missed out on God's beautiful purpose and have hurt themselves because they strayed outside the edges of God's will for them. They sometimes quote the familiar sentence of Philippians 4:13: "I can do all things through Christ who strengthens me,"[4] but forget that this is not a license for doing our own thing whenever we feel like it. We must follow God's leading the way the Israelites followed the divine cloud through the desert, knowing that it will take us where we need to go. As long as the cloud is determining the route, we can be sure that God will fight on our behalf. Otherwise, we are on our own in enemy territory.

Listen to the detail of God's opening promise to Joshua: "Your territory will extend from the desert to Lebanon, and from the great river, the Euphrates—all the Hittite country—to the Mediterranean Sea in the west" (Josh. 1:4). That is an impressive tract of land. In fact, nations and peoples are still fighting over it today, because they want it so badly. But it is not *everything* and *everywhere*. It is a precise allotment for a specific recipient.

And it would not come easily. In the very same conversation God said to Joshua *three times*, "Be strong and courageous" (v. 6). "Be strong and very courageous" (v. 7). "Have I not commanded you? Be strong and courageous. Do not be afraid; do not be discouraged, for the Lord your God will be with you" (v. 9).

> Moving into the land God has waiting for us is not something for the timid or fearful.

This new leader no longer had his beloved mentor, Moses, to lean on. In a sense, it might be said that his "prop" was gone now. The great pioneer of the Exodus from Egypt was no longer around to advise him. Joshua would have to lean on the Lord for the courage and boldness that upcoming battles would require.

Likewise, the "more" that God has for you and me will require courage—no doubt about it. We cannot always depend on those who have supported us in the past. Inevitably, our godly parents die, our Christian friends move away, our situations change. But God's power and faithfulness continue. When we remember that our strength and help come from the Lord, we can stand firm to face the challenges arrayed against us.

Moving into the land God has waiting for us is not

something for the timid or fearful. It is for people who know that God would not bring us this far in life only to drop us into some black hole. After giving his Son for us on the cross, will he now abandon his own children? No, he is a faithful God. As he said through his prophet Isaiah, "I am the LORD; those who hope in me will not be disappointed" (Isa. 49:23). The battles ahead are real and often intense. But if we fight the way God tells us to, and we call upon his name for resources at every turn, we *will* overcome. His promises, when met with our simple faith, cannot be frustrated.

A spacious place is waiting. It's time to step up.

CHAPTER 2

AN ASSIGNMENT JUST FOR YOU

One of the first things to understand about the Promised Land is that it is not simply a place of material blessing. Money, tropical vacations, stock portfolios, good-looking kids who make the honor roll ... none of these does justice to the picture God has in mind. Far too many of us get sidetracked because we only focus on what we might get from God to make us more comfortable.

Nor is the Promised Land a place of getting to relax and do nothing. Yes, many people today are stressed and over-scheduled, wishing for some time off. But if that is your definition of realizing God's favor in your life, you will be disappointed.

Think about this: If I were to spend three days sitting and watching TV for eight hours a day, eating cookies and cheese doodles, I should be well rested, right? I've saved all kinds of energy, since I've hardly budged from my favorite chair.

Actually, the opposite is true. I will get tired just heading up the stairs to go to bed. My life of total leisure has actually sapped me of my strength.

Muscle tone is developed and energy is created not by

doing nothing, but by doing something. This principle holds true in the spiritual realm as well. It is why so many Christians lack the fulfillment and strength God wants them to have. They have not yet found their personal work assignment in God's overall plan, which was conceived by him long before they even became Christians. Their days and weeks lack a sense of individual purpose and drive. They are like the Dead Sea, with fresh water flowing in but nothing flowing out. As a result, the sea is a salty brew of chemicals that nobody wants to drink.

We all know believers who live with a gnawing lack of fulfillment. Something is definitely missing. They often try to fill the void by buying a new book or CD from a Christian personality. They may switch versions of the Bible. They wonder about changing churches. All of these temporarily distract them without getting to the heart of the matter. The key to filling their emptiness is to discover and then carry out their work assignment from the Lord.

> God has called every single Christian to do something special, something mighty, something unique.

God has called every single Christian to do something special, something mighty, something unique that only he or she can do. God knows your personality. He is the source of all your gifts and strengths. He also knows your great potential to advance his kingdom.

God chose Joshua for a unique assignment, and it was a perfect fit. As soon as Joshua received his commission from God, he ordered the officers of the Israelites, "Go through the camp and tell the people, 'Get your provisions ready. Three days from now you will cross the Jordan here to go in and take possession of the land the LORD your God is giving you for your own.'" (Josh. 1:11).

This was the big moment! It signified, "Okay, here we go! This is it! No more sitting around in the desert. Now we get to see God's plan fulfilled for our nation."

And how did the people react? Verse 16 says: "Then they answered Joshua: 'Whatever you have commanded us we will do, and wherever you send us we will go.'" They sounded excited to be on the move at last. Their dreams were about to become reality.

"The Work of the Lord"

This was the Israelites' special assignment from God. The question for each one of us in the twenty-first century is: *What's mine?* What specific thing has God planned for me to accomplish in his name? It is probably not to possess physical real estate, the way Joshua and his people conquered the Promised Land. But what *does* God want you and me to do?

Several verses in the New Testament speak specifically about something called "the work of the Lord," encouraging us to know what it is and then to follow up with diligence. For example: "My dear brothers and sisters, stand firm. Let nothing move you. Always give yourselves fully *to the work of the Lord*, because you know that your labor in the Lord is not in vain" (1 Cor. 15:58). The next chapter mentions Paul's young associate Timothy, who "is *carrying on the work of the Lord*, just as I am" (1 Cor. 16:10).

Near the end of his letter to the Colossians (a church he had never visited but apparently knew something about), Paul included an odd personal note for one person: "Tell Archippus: 'See to it that you *complete the work you have received in the Lord*'" (4:17).

Imagine the drama when this letter was first read in the Colossian church, perhaps by the pastor. People would have been sitting quietly, listening to the apostle's exposition of who Jesus is and how they should serve him. Various doctrinal and practical topics were covered. And then, one man's name was read aloud. If he was present that day, all eyes no doubt turned in his direction. The thrust of the directive was that the Lord had given Archippus a special work to do, a personal calling—and he should keep at it. *Don't quit! Don't slack off. Keep going, Archippus!*

Was he embarrassed? Had he been wavering in some way? Was he distracted by other things in life? We don't know. But it seems that this sentence was an alert of some kind ("See to it"). Completing the work he had received was to be top priority for this individual.

Everyone who has accepted Christ as Savior is an Archippus. We have received a special assignment from our Lord. Now we must stay with it until the mission is accomplished. This takes endurance and determination. It is easy to become discouraged, especially if we don't see quick results. It is tempting to listen to criticism from those who think we're not doing our work the right way. Or the enemy tells us we are inadequate; we don't have what it takes to complete the assignment. We've made too many mistakes already.

Don't believe the lies of Satan! No matter what you have or haven't done up to this point, God wants you to stay the course. He gave you a mission because he knew you could do it. It's always too soon to quit. It's never too late to get started again.

Special Assignments Come from the Lord

Any special assignment for you and me is, first and foremost, God's idea. It is not something we concoct by ourselves. For

Joshua, the assignment was the long-awaited fulfillment of God's mighty promise going back more than four hundred years. God had singled out this territory for his people a long, long time ago. Now he would make it happen. Joshua was simply his lieutenant to get the Israelites organized.

Our assignment, like Joshua's, is focused in some way on carrying out *God's* mission. His grand scheme includes two primary objectives: (1) to spread the gospel to all creation, and (2) to nurture those who receive the gospel so that they grow into spiritual maturity. In sum, it's about *evangelism* and *discipleship*. As Jesus told the Eleven shortly before he left the earth, "Go and make disciples of all nations, baptizing them in the name of the Father and of the Son and of the Holy Spirit, and teaching them to obey everything I have commanded you" (Matt. 28:19-20). The Master's goals are all captured in that one sentence.

These are the things that heaven focuses on. When God looks at you and me, he immediately thinks about how to deploy us in his work of evangelism and discipleship. This is different from one's occupation as a teacher, a plumber, a business leader, a secretary, a sales representative, or a dentist. Those are all roles we *occupy*—hence, the word "occupation." As important as these are, you don't have to be a Christian to do them. A person can be an atheist and a brilliant surgeon at the same time.

God is about something much more active and far-reaching when he gives us our special assignment. He takes teachers, plumbers, secretaries, and all the rest and says to them, "I, the Lord of the universe, have a big job for you to do! You may not think you're cut out for this, but I do. You're going to help bring about a radical change in this world's landscape, as the Israelites did when they invaded Canaan. Just listen to what I have in mind!"

These assignments take many forms. For some of us, the assignment is to sing in a church choir or be a worship leader. For another, it's to serve the elderly. For others, it is to teach a Bible class or raise money for mission work or translate the Scriptures into a new language or comfort the grieving. Some of us are called to do this full-time, while others make time for this alongside secular employment. Each of us has our own task that God has assigned. All of the tasks synchronize to advance his goals.

Joshua's invasion force needed soldiers, spies, blacksmiths, cooks, equipment organizers, trainers, and dozens of other jobs. Every army needs a variety of roles, and each one is important. What God calls us to do is just as strategic. The various assignments all add up to a powerful force that can lead us into the Promised Land.

Whenever I think about fulfilling a special assignment from God, I give thanks for a woman in our church named Marcela Cabrera. She came to New York from her native Panama to study information systems at one of our universities. Soon she was working for Merrill Lynch, and today she is a vice-president with a major bank, carrying huge responsibility for technology business management. Whenever you talk to Marcela, you sense her calm, unflappable, efficient manner. You can just tell that if something needs to get done and done *right*, she's the go-to person for the job.

But the world of high finance is not her "assignment" from the Lord. She is the director of the Brooklyn Tabernacle's hospitality ministry, which serves our constant flow of guest singers, speakers, and visitor groups. This is a big job with lots of details to be covered. Marcela has recruited and trained a team of more than sixty hostesses, whom she has on rotation each month. Recently we have added the area of food service administration, since we are operating a cafeteria for people to enjoy before or after services. We also provide meals in a hospitality suite for guest ministers. All of this runs smoothly under Marcela's leadership.

Then there's the matter of couples preparing for their wedding day. Marcela is the coordinator who helps them figure out what to serve and how, what a realistic budget would look like, and how to make their wedding day special.

But that's not all. This woman helps organize all-church picnics and other special events. She also taught a pilot home economics class for young women (and even some young men) on six Saturday afternoons. "I remember how the godly women of the church back in Panama taught us young girls how to sew, how to cook, how to keep a house," she says. "I guess it's my turn now to pass that kind of knowledge along. Some of these girls really need practical instruction. We even rolled in an actual brass bed to the classroom so I could demonstrate how to make it properly!"

> God takes teachers, plumbers, secretaries, and all the rest and says, "I have a big job for you to do!"

And, oh, yes—in her "spare time" Marcela sings soprano in the Brooklyn Tabernacle Choir.

With all this time-consuming work, she doesn't even have a desk at the church. We did set up an email account for her, which she fields from home.

What does the bank think of all this outside activity? "They're fine about it," she says. "They want everyone to be involved in some kind of community service, helping a nonprofit organization or project. So obviously, the Brooklyn Tabernacle is my 'community service' in their eyes. I put up bits of information on my personal webpage at work—when the choir wins a Grammy award, for example—and my co-workers rejoice with me. When management is looking for somebody to handle the annual March of Dimes campaign in the office, they don't bother asking me; they know I'm already doing my 'community service' quota, and then some."

Marcela Cabrera's "special assignment" from the Lord is critical to the operation of our church. Yes, it utilizes her unique experience in project management, computer programming, and the business meetings she has arranged for her employers not only locally, but in various Latin American hubs (since she's bilingual). But in our mind, she is a gift of God to our ministry for Christ. We don't know what we would do without her joyful contribution of time and energy.

Not everyone's contribution is as far-reaching as Marcela's, to be sure. But whether large or small, each person's assignment serves to advance the divine mission. Everyone is making an impact for the kingdom.

There Are Special Assignments for Everyone

God has a work assignment for *every* Christian, not just those of us who are ordained to pastoral and preaching ministry. The apostle Paul wrote to the Ephesian congregation, "I urge you to live a life worthy of the calling you have received.... *To each one of us* grace has been given as Christ apportioned it" (4:1, 7). Later he adds, "From him [Christ] the whole body, joined and held together by every *supporting* ligament, grows and builds itself up in love, *as each part does its work*" (v. 16).

Receiving Christ into our lives is not the end of something, but the beginning. The next step is to receive and carry out our special assignment. Unfortunately, in too many places Christianity has been reduced to mere mental assent to a list of doctrines. Others have had a genuine salvation experience, but their daily Christian life is now little more than attending a service once a week. Jesus has far more in mind for us than this.

When Joshua organized the invasion of Canaan, he didn't just speak to the priests—the religious leaders. He didn't just call a meeting of all the men ages 18 to 35. He included the entire community, "the people" (Josh. 1:10). No one was exempted.

Not even the fighting men of Reuben, Gad, and the half-tribe of Manasseh got off the hook. These tribes had already received their homesteads east of the Jordan following a previous victory. They could well have begged off from having to join any additional campaign. But in Joshua 1:12–15, the commander said to them, in essence, "You too! Come on with the rest of us. You have a part to play here. Once we take possession of this territory west of the river, then you can go back home. Not before."

God's mission to spread his gospel around the world and raise up mature disciples is an all-hands-on-deck enterprise. Each one of us has an assignment to fulfill. None of us can just assume that "they" (whoever "they" are) will take care of the need. Everyone has a part to play. We may not think our contribution is all that valuable. But that is wrong. God makes the assignment, not us. And he knows how vital each part is. "God has placed the parts in the body, every one of them, just as he wanted them to be" (1 Cor. 12:18).

Many years ago, a modest man of God in England (he never wrote under his full name, but only with his initials, E.D.) made this observation: "We are slow to learn that the importance of any service depends upon God's estimate of it ... that the meanest [lowest-ranking] service ... is worthy of all our devotedness and zeal if the mind and heart of God are upon it, and if He has put it into our hand."[1]

You have a far more strategic role to play than just filling a church pew and helping to meet the annual budget. God has an assignment designed precisely for you—and this is part of the abundant life you so earnestly crave. As you give yourself to God's special assignment, you will pray more and with a deeper sense of passion. You will hunger for a greater understanding of the Bible and how it applies to your life. You will regularly sense the help of the Holy Spirit, since God always works *with* those who give themselves to work *for* him.

If, by contrast, we sadly reduce our relationship with God to a preoccupation with "bless me, bless me," we will only be frustrated. The more we reach for happiness in life, the more it eludes us. The more we try to fill our emptiness with cars, clothes, and cruises, the deeper the vacuum, since none of those things meets the spiritual craving within. God made us to find true joy through knowing and serving him. We were redeemed from our old self-centeredness to channel God's love and grace to others while bringing glory to the person of Jesus Christ. That is what our assignment is all about.

Special Assignments Will Definitely Stretch You

Joshua encountered many unexpected crises as he led the Israelites into Canaan. On one occasion he had to repudiate a man named Achan, who stole some sacred items and caused God to bring a military defeat as punishment. At another time Joshua had to confront a nearby tribe, the Gibeonites, who had lied in order to get a peace treaty. He may have felt quite unprepared for situations like these—but he was determined to do what God had called him to do.

God's kingdom will not be achieved by halfhearted measures. When we begin to act on our special assignment, it is pretty much guaranteed that we will be pushed beyond our comfort zones. We may be called to do things we don't feel prepared for, even if we are capable. The assignment may call for more faith and courage than we have ever known.

> The more we try to fill our emptiness with cars, clothes, and cruises, the deeper the vacuum, since none of those things meets the craving within.

Some of the most fulfilling moments of my life were the Sunday nights in the church's previous building when I had to crawl home after four services almost too exhausted to change out of my suit. Today, with the larger building God has provided, we are accommodating the need with just three services. It still takes a toll on the body, particularly my voice. Yet, a well of joy rises up from getting to serve others in the name of Christ. I fall into bed saying, "Thank you, Lord, for the chance to make a difference in somebody's life today."

Isn't it interesting that at the very end of Paul's life, he wrote in 2 Timothy 4:7, "I have fought the good fight," not "I've had a nice vacation"?

Yes, we can all benefit from a getaway occasionally. But my wife, Carol, and I have noticed that after a few days we are both happy to get back to choir rehearsals and sermon preparation and prayer meetings and helping people find jobs and all the rest that goes with the ministry. It is amazing how boring it can be to sit beside a swimming pool when the work of God beckons.

Francis Asbury, who was sent by John Wesley to guide the Methodist awakening in America, said to his young ministers in training, "Though the devil attacks you in a thousand ways and though there are problems on every side, you are never happier than when you are in the work of the Lord." This from a man who was never in good health and yet traveled nearly 300,000 miles during his ministry, mostly on horseback. He even stayed on the American side of the Atlantic through the entire Revolutionary War—the only English Methodist leader to do so.

One of the couples in our church who has been willing to stretch for God's purposes is Mark and Georgina Hill. Mark is a licensed architect and a very good one. When he graduated from Cornell University in the mid-1980s, he found his first job to be less than challenging, so he boldly put in his application to work for the very best: I. M. Pei, the world-famous mind who has created everything from the John F. Kennedy Library (Boston) to the Pyramids of the Louvre (Paris) to the Rock and Roll Hall of Fame (Cleveland). Mark got the job and absolutely loved it. The freshness, the creativity, the bold strokes were inspiring.

Then Mark took a beginner course in children's ministry at the Brooklyn Tabernacle. This kindled something he had long cared about. "Growing up as a pastor's son, I hated Sunday school; it was the most boring thing around. Now as an adult, it bothered me whenever I'd visit a church somewhere and see kids sleeping in the back row or scribbling on paper. I wanted to make a difference."

Mark, still single at this point, began finding time to teach the elementary-age children's church. "I loved it! I had such a feeling of being in God's will. And the kids responded so energetically."

Along the way he got to meet one of the preschool-level teachers: Georgina, a district manager of seventeen women's clothing stores. The little children in her Sunday class graduated each year into Mark's group. The two adults found out they had more common interests, and in time they were married.

"While Mark seemed called especially to the church-wise kid, the one who had grown up in church and heard all the Bible stories," says Georgina, "I developed a tender heart for the marginalized child, the one who wasn't dressed quite as nice as the others, who felt uneasy in the group. I began making a point of calling that child by name several times during the hour, just to see the smile come up on the face."

Georgina then came across a book that changed her life: *Unlocking the Secret World: A Unique Christian Ministry to Abused, Abandoned, and Neglected Children* by Wayne and Diane Tesch.[2] She was riveted with the horrors of what some kids endure. She was stunned by a *New York Daily News* story about a seven-year-old boy who was found wrapped in duct tape like a mummy and lying in a bathtub of cold water because his mother's boyfriend had gotten upset with him. When the police rescued him and unwrapped his little body, they found bruises everywhere. Hardened NYPD officers wept at the sight.

Georgina picked up the phone and called Wayne Tesch simply to thank him for writing the book. He could sense her interest and arranged to meet the couple when he came to New York. Before long, Mark and Georgina went out to California at their own expense for a ten-day training session with Tesch's organization, Royal Family Kids Camp (RFKC). This program provides a safe week of summer camping for abused children, with lavish care and fun as well as appropriate teaching about God's love. The training happened at a campground during an actual camping week.

"The Lord broke our hearts together," Georgina says. "We

would go back to our room and just cry. We knew we had to try to launch one of these camps in the New York area."

It took several years and several false starts before, in 1999, the first thirty children went to a rented facility in the Pocono Mountains of eastern Pennsylvania. It was a huge success. The next year, the Hills were able to invite more kids, based on referrals from the New York City Department of Social Services. Dozens of adult workers from the church joined them in ministering to these precious children. They even thought of throwing a mass birthday party for *all* the kids — the first party and first birthday present some of them had ever known.

Today Mark and Georgina collect money to take a hundred kids to camp each summer — and they are not satisfied. "Pastor Cymbala, we want to figure out how to acquire a camp of our own," they say. "Not that we're asking the church to buy it. We just think God could provide it from another source. If we had that, we could run lots of camps!"

They talk intensely about how hard it is for single parents who are at risk of losing their children to state custody. "Social Services says you have to go to a six-week class and do all the homework, or they'll take your kids away," they tell me. "Well, do they provide babysitting? Of course not. If the mom leaves her kids alone in the apartment while she goes to class, she's in even deeper trouble. She can't win.

"But if we had a camp ... we could load up buses full of these families and take them out to Connecticut or Pennsylvania for a whole weekend. We could have licensed teachers cover all the material Social Services wants — even give the official certificate — and in the meantime, we could do fun activities with the kids, build in family mealtimes with good food, and have a gospel presentation. It would be awesome!" Their mental wheels are turning fast as they talk.

This dream has not yet become a reality for Mark and Georgina. But they are doing everything they can think of to bring it to pass. They have started an impressive Christian bookstore, called Timeless Treasures, right around the corner from the church, hoping that its proceeds will someday advance the camp dream for abused children.

All of this has required tons of time. They have a son of their own, Ryan, who is now in middle school. And what about Mark's architectural career? In 2006 he went to the firm's partners and asked for a sabbatical. They responded, "Well, Mark, you've been with our company for eleven years now. You've never let us down. You're doing a great job on the current project. As long as your client doesn't complain, keep going. Do the work whenever you can fit it in. We don't mind if you're not in the office every day."

That worked for a while. But Mark felt he needed more time to manage the Royal Family Kids Camp work and also help Georgina with the bookstore. After a long process of thought and prayer, he went back to the partners a second time about some kind of change.

> God's calling for each Christian may end up being broader and more complex than any of us imagine in the beginning.

"We don't want to lose you," they said. "Would you be willing to continue as a consultant for us?"

That is Mark's current arrangement. His six-figure salary is gone now. He earns only what he can bill by the hour. And still he is a happy man. He is functioning within his special assignment from the Lord. So is his wife.

I can tell you that this is the opposite of what usually happens. What ministers normally hear these days is, "Well, Pastor, I just got a promotion at work, with more travel, and so I'm going to need to stop teaching Sunday school now.

Gotta make a living, you know." In this case, Mark is saying, "Well, Boss, I really want to spend more time helping kids in distress, so I guess I need to go off the formal payroll." Talk about a different value system!

A wise marriage counselor wrote some years ago to couples,

> To try to keep love just for us ... is to kill it slowly.... We are not made just for each other; we are called to a ministry of love to everyone we meet and in all we do. In marriage, too, Jesus' words hold true: in saving our lives we lose them, and in losing our lives in love to others, we drink of life more deeply.[3]

God's calling for each Christian may end up being broader and more complex than any of us imagine in the beginning. That's all right. When he stretches us to new frontiers, he grants his provision to meet our needs, and he gives us fresh energy to succeed. He is bringing us into a new and spacious land that far outstrips the past.

What Is *Your* Special Assignment?

If you are not sure what your special assignment from God is, go to him in prayer and ask him. Stay with it and pray until you receive direction. Surrender your will and life to the Lord. He will not only lead you, but also provide the wisdom and resources needed.

Archippus was reminded to *complete* the work assignment he had obviously already begun. Possibly something or someone had distracted or discouraged him. This often happens when we set ourselves wholeheartedly to do the work of the Lord. But God will continue faithfully to complete his purpose as we keep our eyes on Christ.

As God leads and equips us, we will experience the most exciting and fulfilling life here on earth. We will see prayers answered, people forever changed, and the rise of a new spiritual energy within us. Enemies of every kind will be driven out, and the good land God has promised will be ours. We can start to go after it today, never forgetting the fact that God made us for so much more.

THE PLACE
OF GOD'S BLESSING

If you were a television news editor putting together a one-hour special on the invasion of Canaan, you would naturally choose the most dramatic footage your film crews had shot. You would lead off, no doubt, with Joshua's army storming across the Jordan River after it had amazingly parted in front of them. You would spend a good block of time on the week of marching around Jericho and the thunderous collapse of its walls. You might include the momentary setback at Ai, due to sin in the camp. But soon you would be back to more military "shock and awe," as more cities fell to the advancing Israelites. Your grand finale would be when God helped Joshua and his troops by unleashing a violent hailstorm on the enemy—hard enough to cause casualties—and then even lending them extra daylight hours so they could finish the battle.

Would the news editor then look at the religious ceremonies at Gilgal (Josh. 4–5)? Nah! Too dull. TV audiences go for *action*. Keep the tension building—never let it sag. That's the way you hold viewers.

I admit I never paid much attention to Gilgal either, until

I ran across an obscure mention further down the time line, in Judges 2. By now, Joshua had passed away, and the Israelites were quickly drifting away from God. The opening line of the chapter says, "The angel of the LORD went up from Gilgal to Bokim...."

Why would the Bible bother to tell us where the angel of the Lord came *from?* Most other references in Scripture simply say that God's special angel shows up at a certain place (on Mount Horeb with the discouraged Elijah, for example, or at the spring in the desert where Hagar stopped for water). The angel of the Lord gives his message, then disappears. Where the angel comes from goes unmentioned.

But Gilgal, a small place a mile or two northeast of Jericho, apparently held some kind of spiritual significance. God was present there in a unique way. Even hundreds of years after Joshua led the invasion of the land, the prophet Samuel repeatedly returned to Gilgal to offer sacrifices, to confront King Saul about his wayward deeds, to call the nation to renewed dedication. This practice stemmed, I believe, from what God did in this place back in Joshua's day.

Gilgal was the Israelites' first stop after crossing the Jordan; it became their "base camp" for launching many military forays. It was also a training ground where God taught his people three lessons that made future victories possible. These three principles remain significant for us today. They make up a set of keys to God's abiding presence and blessing. We dare not push ahead on the Israelites' story without looking at the lessons of Gilgal.

1. Look Back before You Move Forward

At Gilgal, Joshua followed God's command to take twelve large stones from the middle of the Jordan River—which

God had miraculously divided to allow his people to cross on dry land—and set them up as memorial stones. The purpose of the stones was to spark discussions with the next generation: "In the future, when your children ask you, 'What do these stones mean?' tell them that the flow of the Jordan was cut off before the ark of the covenant of the LORD" (Josh. 4:6–7). In this way the miracle of God's power and provision would be reinforced.

These stones were not idols to be worshiped. Rather, they were testimonials to the faithfulness of the one and only God. They gave reason to give God praise. And in such a climate, "the angel of the Lord" felt right at home.

> We would do well not to focus on the troubles lined up against us. Instead, we need to celebrate the God who has already demonstrated his power and provision in our past.

When the people of Israel looked out toward the perimeter of their camp, they might naturally have wondered how many Canaanite armies were lurking in the shadows or behind walls, waiting to harm them. But when they focused on the twelve stones, their fears evaporated. Their God had just stopped the flood-stage Jordan so they could cross over! Surely he could stop the arrows and rocks of the enemy, too.

In our confrontations with obstacles or opponents today, we would do well not to focus on the troubles lined up against us. Instead, we need to celebrate the God who has already demonstrated his power and provision in our past. We don't need to be fretful or anxious. We need to anchor our hearts and minds in God's overwhelming track record.

The Bible says, "Come near to God and he will come near to you" (James 4:8). Apparently not all Christians live the same distance from God. Even though we all belong to his family, some are pressing in closer to his dynamic strength than others. As we live a life full of praise and thanksgiving for past mercies, we experience God coming ever closer to us in the present.

Psalm 22:3 speaks about God being "enthroned upon the praises of Israel."[1] What a difference it would make if we simply paused once an hour or so to say, "I praise you, Lord. You've been so good to me! I give you thanks." Just think how much more joy and peace would be ours all day long.

This would be valuable not only on sunny days but also in times of testing and loss. Of course, problems come our way throughout life. That is inevitable. But instead of worrying, we can face the difficulties in a context of all that God has done for us in the past. When our backs were against the wall, God opened a door of provision. He is the same God today.

George Müller ran an orphanage in Bristol, England, in the 1800s that served more than 100,000 children over a fifty-year period. He said God had led him not to solicit any funds for this work. Instead, he would just trust and wait. As a result, his walk of faith and prayer grew dramatically. One New Year's Eve, when he was fifty-nine years old, he said in a sermon,

> We have, through the goodness of the Lord, been permitted to enter upon another year—and the minds of many among us will no doubt be occupied with plans for the future, and the various fears of our work and service for the Lord.... Above all things see to it that your souls are *happy in the Lord*. Other things may press upon you, the Lord's work may even have urgent claims upon your attention, but I deliberately repeat, it is of supreme and paramount importance that you should seek above all things to have your souls truly *happy in God Him-*

self! Day by day seek to make this the most important business of your life. This has been my firm and settled condition for the last five and thirty years.[2]

Be "happy in God" on the basis of his faithfulness up to now—that is the first lesson of Gilgal. Naturally we will face challenges, but let us not major in them. Rather, let us major in thanksgiving for the blessings God has already poured out on our lives. The one who brought us out of our "Egypt," who forgave our sins and made us his own, will not fail us now.

> Certainly each Christian has at least twelve memorials to God's goodness from a past day. Some of us have 12,000!

Worry changes nothing. God wants us instead to look at the twelve stones in our lives. Certainly each Christian has at least twelve memorials to God's goodness from a past day when we've really needed him. Some of us have 12,000!

A whole cluster of memorial stones of praise in my life comes from the way God brought our church to its present location on Smith Street. After what we have lived through the past few years, you will never convince me that God is not a God of miracle provision. We were so cramped in the old building on Flatbush Avenue. We were holding three services a Sunday in a converted theater that could seat 1,200. People were having to sit in overflow rooms watching the service on TV monitors. Our children and youth were jammed into basement rooms far too small.

One Sunday afternoon in 1996 as I walked toward the sanctuary for the 3:30 service, I happened upon a woman trying to sign in her seven-year-old son for children's church. I overheard the worker say, "I'm so sorry, but we are just totally filled up. There's no room for your boy."

I watched that mother as her shoulders sagged. She would have to take her son along with her to the lobby instead and watch the service on a TV monitor. If the child became restless, she would miss part of the benefit—and meanwhile, the boy would miss getting to learn about Jesus at an appropriate level. I felt a great sadness. All through that afternoon service I couldn't get that woman and her son out of my mind.

"God, this shouldn't happen," I said silently. "This is the Lord's house. Somebody who goes to the work of taking maybe two different subway trains to get here should have the opportunity to worship you unhindered, and her child should be taught and loved. What are we going to do about this?"

That week I met with the pastors and described what I had seen. We began to pray, "God, this can't be your will for people to be turned away. What do you have in mind?" We took a number of days to seek the Lord. We came to the conclusion that while God had blessed us abundantly in this building, its time was now over. Something *more* was in his future for us. What might it be?

We didn't know, but we did know that something had to change right away, even temporarily. Until we could get to a bigger place, the leadership decided to add yet another service. We would now have church at 9 a.m., 12 noon, 3 p.m., and 6 p.m. on Sunday. With each service running around two hours, this would make for a marathon day. But we could stand anything for a couple of years, we told ourselves.

Little did we know that it would be *six* years before we "entered the Promised Land." We knocked on a lot of doors and went down several blind alleys until finally God led us to the historic Loew's Metropolitan Theater in the heart of downtown Brooklyn, which had a glorious history but was now terribly dilapidated. Water had damaged its once-beautiful neoclassical ceiling. The plumbing, heating, and electrical systems were a disaster. Homeless alcoholics and drug addicts had been using it for shelter. Some of the rats were large enough to be carrying attaché cases with *The New York Times* tucked under one arm!

Yes, it seated 4,100 when built back in 1918, the largest theater in North America at that time. Besides the auditorium, the parcel now included three adjacent office buildings. So the potential was huge. And the location was marvelous, right at the convergence of multiple subway and bus lines. All we needed was money—lots of it.

And we had none. Plus, ours was not a rich, suburban congregation. This was an inner-city church of many hourly-wage earners, students, single parents, and a fair number of unemployed. I knew better than to ask for pledges of large amounts. Nor did I want to disenfranchise anyone. So I decided to take a once-a-month offering for the project, asking our people to think about a fifty-dollar gift. The rest, I knew, would have to come from outside sources.

About this time, I was invited to an interview on *The 700 Club* regarding my first book, *Fresh Wind, Fresh Fire*. Host Pat Robertson asked me how things were going at the church. I shared with him our situation, and he said he would like to help in some way. The following week, I was shocked to receive a letter from him promising $1 million! I hadn't asked him directly for any amount of money.

We took this as a "memorial stone"—a provision of God that meant we should move forward. Our faith began to swell. I went to the theater owners with a bold offer of $6.3 million in cash. They accepted.

In a short amount of time God supplied the balance needed, and the property became ours. We felt exhilarated.

We thought our journey of faith was complete. That was before we began seriously tallying the cost of renovation.

We were soon reminded that, this being New York City, the job would have to involve union contractors every step of the way. Electricians, for example, made $90 an hour. It was especially galling to walk through the job site and find some of them smoking pot during working hours. At one point we faced a demand to hire an additional worker who was, in our view, completely unneeded. But we had no options. The unions held the power to shut the entire project down at any time. They also darkly warned about mysterious "accidents" to the building that could happen in the middle of the night.

I remember once when our finance manager informed me that we needed another $600,000 within forty-eight hours or else the work would have to stop. My wife, Carol, was away that day caring for her mother, who was ill. The Lord impressed me that morning not to go into the office as usual; instead, I should seek his help in a little prayer room we have in our attic.

I stayed in the attic from ten in the morning until around five-thirty in the afternoon, calling out to God to show himself as our strong provider. During those hours a number of phone calls and other messages came in—providing enough to meet our need that week.

This was not the only time such a last-minute provision took place. One time we had to come up with $1.4 million within two weeks. The Lord rose up to help us. At another time the figure was $6 million to complete Phase One of the renovation. I came back from a ministry trip to South America and began going through a stack of mail that had accumulated while I was away. Within ten minutes I opened one envelope pledging $1 million—and another for $5 million! I had no idea that either of those gifts was coming.

We moved into the new facility in May 2002, scaling back to "just" three services a Sunday, now that the building could accommodate larger crowds. It has turned out to be a marvelous center for ministry. We could never have imagined all the blessings God had in store for us in this place. Every time I walk into the building, look up at the beautifully restored ceilings, or hear the air conditioning kick on, I am reminded of God's faithfulness. What an amazing memorial stone he has provided!

Plus, the value of this property has soared in the wake of the 9/11 tragedy. New York City lost hundreds of thousands of square feet of office space that terrible day. Many a corporation has since looked toward downtown Brooklyn to relocate their workers. Then a major developer named Bruce Ratner bought the New Jersey Nets professional basketball team and decided to build them a new home in Brooklyn. The new complex, called the Atlantic Yards—just six blocks from our church—will include an 18,000-seat sports arena plus two huge office buildings, condos, and other commercial space with an overall price tag of $4.1 *billion*. All of this is driving real estate values higher.

> Outsiders have commented, "You guys must be real estate geniuses! You jumped into the market at just the right moment." No, we didn't have a clue.

Had we built this church from the ground up, we would have been required to buy an extra square block just for parking, at an astronomical price. But because the building was formerly a theater—a place of public assembly—we were spared this regulation. We don't need that much parking anyway, since more than half of the congregation comes via public transit.

In sum, outsiders have commented, "You guys must be real estate geniuses! You jumped in at just the right moment." No, we didn't have a clue. All we knew was that God wanted us to provide more capacity for his work, and he would be faithful to make it possible. He certainly has been!

I don't expect to face this particular kind of construction project again in my lifetime. But I'm sure other challenges will come along. And when they do, I will look back at the pile of "memorial stones" that have accumulated and will say, "Remember how God met those huge needs in the past? He will do it again. He is the God who provides for his people."

If we forget the past victories, we succumb to a kind of spiritual amnesia. How much better to resist the prevailing fear and anxiety with a joyful, positive, thankful outlook. As we remember and celebrate God's goodness, we see the next blessing start to emerge from right around the corner. We move forward with assurance.

2. Don't Try to Move Forward in Disobedience

The second lesson of Gilgal shows up in chapter 5 of the book of Joshua. The generation that had come out of Egypt had forgotten something along the way. During the forty years they spent wandering in the desert, they stopped practicing the sign of the covenant God made with Abraham, Isaac, and Jacob. That sign was circumcision. To be a Hebrew male meant being circumcised. But as sons were born during the wilderness wanderings, God's people failed to honor their covenant obligations. So now God said, in essence, "Stop everything. The present generation is living in disobedience. Don't take another step until you straighten this out."

Joshua initiated a massive circumcision program over the next few days. When it was finished, the Lord responded, "Today I have rolled away the reproach of Egypt from you" (5:9). In fact, that is how the place got its name; "Gilgal" sounds like the Hebrew word for "roll" or "rolling." Gilgal was where the Israelites rolled into alignment with God's requirements, so he could then bless them in the battles that lay ahead.

This relationship between obedience and God's favor is something we don't talk about much today. We prefer to say that God is love, and we are Christians, so we're just going to stand on the promises of his faithfulness, regardless of our lifestyles. We expect God to shower his blessings on us, even though we cheat on the job or harbor bitterness in our hearts. We don't think God would actually withhold his goodness just because of how we live. Come on, nobody's perfect, right?

I am not saying that God will refuse to help us or work through us unless we are sinless. In fact, no one lives a perfect moral life. But there is a major difference between the person who sincerely wants to live like Christ but falls short at times, and the person who persistently disobeys the Bible. For such a person as the latter to cry out in a time of emergency, "O God, O God, help me please!" is a form of hypocrisy.

More than once God has convicted me of some kind of disobedience, such as a heart attitude. On a few Sunday mornings in the past, Carol and I have had "words" with each other on the way to church. Then as the first service began, and I stood there singing along with the congregation and hearing Carol play the keyboard, I have known that I had better not even go up and try to make announcements, let alone preach. Instead, I have walked over to the band pit and simply whispered to her, "I'm sorry for what I said this morning." She has graciously nodded as she continued to play.

At other times I am reading the Word in my devotional time when God puts a finger on my disobedience, saying to me, *You've got to let that go*. Whenever this happens, I cannot brush it aside. I have to deal with whatever God has pointed out.

God directs his children to "walk in the light, as he is in the light" (1 John 1:7). Again, this does not equate to moral perfection. But it does mean being willing to be transparent and sincere. It also means repenting when God points out disobedience, as he did to the nation at Gilgal. If we choose to persist in sin, we have no assurance that God will bless us. He is not our puppet. His grace does not give us license to live however we want. He expects from us devotion and submission to his Word.

I was preaching on this subject at a prayer conference in a western state, and when I got to this point, I said, "Everything stopped before the Israelites could head into the battle against Jericho, because God said, 'No, you can't go. The generation that has come out of Egypt has not been circumcised.' That was the mark God gave to Abraham. It marked him and his family as belonging to God.

"In the same way, we cannot live in known disobedience and expect that God will bless and help us. If he did, he would be encouraging our rebellion. We can't have God and, at the same time, hold onto the sin he sent his Son to die for."

It was a clear enough point to understand. But in that moment I sensed I had somehow totally lost the audience. A wall had gone up—a wall of misunderstanding, I assumed.

People just stared at me. They showed none of the zeal from ten minutes before.

Uh-oh, I said to myself. *There's a disconnect here. They're not with me anymore. I must not have explained it right, and now they're confused.* So in my heart I whispered, *Lord, help me to explain this better. They're not getting it. I must have done a bad job.*

I backed up and went through the point again. I quoted Psalm 66:18: "If I had cherished sin in my heart, the Lord *would not have listened.*" After all, this was a prayer conference. Getting God to listen to us was the main agenda, right?

The more I talked, the stonier the crowd became. I began to realize something. This was not a wall of misunderstanding after all. This was a wall of rejection. This audience did not want to hear that you had to give up anything or adjust anything in your personal life to comply with God's will.

I sputtered a little bit. They wanted to hear that Jesus would meet them wherever they were — and let them stay that way. He shouldn't try to move them to any different kind of lifestyle. They wanted Jesus, but on their terms.

> The more I talked, the stonier the crowd became. I began to realize that this was not a wall of misunderstanding after all. This was a wall of rejection.

I stepped back. *God, is this for real?* I prayed silently. *I feel like I'm in a battle here.*

I then leaned forward again and said, "Maybe some of you think you can live in sin, you can lie on the job, you can sleep around — and still press a button to get 'instant God.' It doesn't work that way.

"If you think I came all the way out here from New York City to get your applause and tell you what you want to hear, you've got the wrong speaker tonight. Whatever you might feel about me personally, I must tell you the truth, or I will fail God miserably."

The place was totally silent. No amens. No nothing.

"You cannot have sin and have God's blessing at the same time. That is what Gilgal means. They could have claimed, 'Yeah, but we're the children of Abraham, Isaac, and Jacob.' Biologically that was true—but their vertical relationship with God was messed up." I kept on imploring them with this thought. "Do you understand? Do you get what I'm saying?"

I paused again. Nothing but more silence. Everyone felt awkward, including me.

Suddenly, from the back of the auditorium a man cried out, "Don't stop! Don't be afraid! You're right—we need to hear this!" His voice was cracking with tears. "Keep going! Say it!"

That was all I needed to turn me loose. I plunged with full force into restating the point. Only then did I sense a bit of breaking in the crowd.

I then moved on to the last point, about the Israelites observing Passover at Gilgal (Josh. 5:10–12). I quoted 1 John 1:9: "If we confess our sins, he is faithful and just and will forgive us our sins and purify us from all unrighteousness."

I said, "God is not trying to rain on your parade. He simply knows that some things to which we're drawn can destroy us. My daughter Susie went through a phase as a little girl where she loved matches and knives. I had to step in and say, No!

"Your holiest days will be your happiest days. The people of Israel got right with God at Gilgal, and they were thereby prepared to go out and conquer the land."

Toward the end of that conference session, I went back

to my hotel. I found my shirt drenched with perspiration, as if I had been in a fistfight. I battled with bewilderment and discouragement.

The next morning, a driver came to pick me up early to catch my flight home. On the way to the airport, I spotted a Target store. "Could we stop here just a minute so I could find something to take to my grandson?" I asked. He pulled into the lot.

I was going down the aisle looking for something an eight-year-old boy would like when a man in his twenties passed the other way. Suddenly he called out, "Jim Cymbala!"

I stopped. "Yes?" I responded.

"Hey! I was there last night when you spoke."

"Oh."

"That was really powerful," he said. "What you preached about Gilgal really got through to my mother."

"Yes?" I said, curious to learn more.

"She was there; she's a believer. She said something interesting to me afterward—that your message spoke to her so much she's going to start praying about leaving the boyfriend she's living with."

"What?" I couldn't quite believe what I'd just heard.

He repeated himself. "She's living with this guy. And she's going to start praying about moving out."

I reached out and grabbed the young man's arm. "Sir," I said with dead seriousness, "I want you to do something the minute you leave this store. I want you to call your mother, tell her you happened to run into me, and give her this message from me: *Do not pray about a single thing in this case. That would be tempting God. Just move out! You don't need to pray about things that God has already called sin.*"

He looked at me with surprise. "Okay, I'll tell her," he answered, hoping I would let go of his arm.

I left the store after buying a little sweatshirt for my grandson and headed back to the waiting car. All the while I was asking myself how far this bizarre attitude was spreading among churchgoers across our nation.

Other ministers have told me that this kind of thinking is not all that unusual among people these days. Some televangelists, in fact, are now aggravating this problem by their practice of avoiding the word *sin* at all costs. Why, you ask? Because the ratings gurus advise them that whenever you tell viewers they should stop doing something, they quickly click to a different channel. They don't want to hear it.

Not long ago two Jewish businessmen here in Brooklyn, a father and son, sat in my office discussing a real estate transaction. They are both very kind men and very successful in the business world. Since they were talking to a Christian minister, they told me how much they both liked to watch a certain popular television preacher.

"Why is that?" I asked.

"He's so good! You know, in our lives, we're into two things: money and family. That's all we live for. And this preacher has a lot of things to say about being good to your family. He also says you can follow certain principles from the book of Proverbs and make a lot of money. So he's right on our wavelength!"

My heart sagged as I thought of a vast audience hardly ever hearing the message the apostle Paul "declared to both Jews and Greeks that they must turn to God in repentance and have faith in our Lord Jesus" (Acts 20:21). Compare that with the contemporary view that says, "Don't tell the people they're doing anything wrong. If you do, they might leave. And nothing justifies turning people off."

Holding back is not the method of our Savior. John 6 tells about a time Jesus spoke, and people decided not to follow him anymore. But he didn't run after them to say, "Well, fellows, I can change that after all. I'm sorry—did that offend you? I must have had a momentary lapse there. Let me fix things up for you."

Gilgal is about facing the need to repent when we sin. It is about yielding our will to God's will and his ways. It is about giving him reason to smile upon us and open up a channel to bless us.

If I have a sinful area in my life and I won't let it go, I cannot appeal with any amount of faith for God to help me in another area of my life. God's special love for us as his sons and daughters includes his chastening us when we fall into a pattern of disobedience. This results in a loss of peace, not to mention a loss of power for the next battle.

Long ago in the fourth century, a teacher and prolific hymn writer known as Ephrem the Syrian observed with great wisdom, "He who will not serve the Lord alone must be the slave of many masters."[3] To reject God's requirements does not set us free to enjoy our independence. It instead plunges us into ever more complicated bondages.

God lovingly calls us to obedience. He never gives up. The fact of his holiness cannot be compromised. When we disobey him, we hurt ourselves and we break communication with him. Only when this is restored can we realize his blessing on our efforts.

3. The Blood Sacrifice Must Always Remain Central

One more thing happened at Gilgal. "On the evening of the fourteenth day of the month ... the Israelites celebrated the Passover. The day after the Passover, that very day, they ate some of the produce of the land: unleavened bread and roasted grain" (Josh. 5:10–11).

Passover celebrated God's provision and protection. The Hebrew people smeared lamb's blood on their doorposts to recall the final plague back in Egypt, when the firstborn of their oppressors died while their own children lived. God had declared, "When I see the blood, I will pass over you. No destructive plague will touch you when I strike Egypt" (Exod. 12:13).

Only the blood of Jesus Christ, shed on the cross two thousand years ago, shields us from the awful judgment of God for sin. We are not justified because of our good intentions. We are not protected because of our tearful appeals. We can, in fact, do nothing to merit God's favor. Only the blood puts us in right standing with him. In the words of the Andraé Crouch song that we often sing in our church, the blood of Jesus "reaches to the highest mountain" and "flows to the lowest valley." That is why "it will never lose its power."[4]

We often take time at the Brooklyn Tabernacle to have people tell and retell the stories of how God reached down to rescue them at their most frightening moments. We never get tired of these testimonies. We never take them for granted. In fact, they create great joy throughout the congregation. We rejoice in the same things that bring joy to the heart of God. Some of these stories come from our own members, others from special guests whom we invite to come our way. I want our members always to stay mindful of the fact that "the blood of Jesus, [God's] Son, purifies us from all sin" (1 John 1:7).

More than once we have welcomed Fernando Aranda from California to recount his amazing journey from hopelessness to Christ. He grew up in the rough barrios of East Los Angeles, the youngest of five children. From his earliest years, the pull of the streets and the allure of drugs proved more powerful than any home influence. He began sniffing glue and running with older gang members while still in grade school. In fact, he was a chronic truant by age eight, which resulted in a three-year stint at a boys' reformatory.

By age eleven he returned to the violent neighborhood and joined a dangerous gang. He and a friend soon got arrested for hitting a man over the head with a crowbar. That landed "Fernie," as he was known, in another camp situation for troubled juveniles. He returned to the streets two years later as a young teenager totally out of control.

> We are not justified because of our good intentions or tearful appeals. We can in fact do nothing to merit God's favor.

As he neared his sixteenth birthday, Fernie made two interesting decisions: to get serious about a girlfriend (a pastor's daughter, no less), and to try to join the Marines! Both his grandfather and father had served in that branch of the military. In Fernie's case, neither arrangement worked very well. "My problem in the Marines," he says today with a smile, "was that there was no war going on just then! So I fought anybody who was around. I got busted five times for insubordination." Soon he was pushed out of the service.

Meanwhile, he so provoked his teenage wife by his wild lifestyle that she shot him in the hand one day with a 25-millimeter weapon. She then took their baby daughter and left.

Fernie, however, was not about to straighten up. He met an older man nicknamed "Folsom Eddie" (from his long residence at that particular California prison), who offered Fernie a chance to make quick money. Their business would be bank robbery and kidnapping. All Fernie had to do was drive the getaway car.

Fernie's second wife, Donna, didn't mind this kind of activity at all. She was as enchanted with drugs and guns as her husband, and in fact, sported more tattoos than he did. She did get upset, however, the night she followed her husband to a party and caught him dancing with another girl. She stabbed him in the back with a knife.

Folsom Eddie and Fernie managed their biggest score when they nabbed a bank president and wound up with a quarter-million dollars, which they split. Eddie, however, spent a good deal of his take in L.A. bars bragging about his exploits. Soon the police picked up the scent and started looking for both men.

Early one morning, Fernie and Donna came to visit their baby, who was being cared for by Fernie's mother. Neither of them expected the police to be waiting. They had wiretapped his mother's phone. It wasn't long before the young man was packed off to a northern California prison with a twenty-five-years-to-life sentence.

Fernie's rebellion continued even behind bars. When three inmates were murdered in the prison yard, Fernie was one of a handful of suspects put into solitary confinement. For twenty-three hours a day he saw nothing but his cell. At the monthly investigation meetings about the killings, he would only mutter, "I don't know nuthin'."

Then came the day that his frail little mother, seventy-one years old, arrived to visit him. The sight of her son in full shackles, shuffling slowly toward the phone on the other side of the bulletproof glass, made her burst into tears. "I don't want to die seeing you in this condition," she cried. All too soon, the visiting hour was over.

Fernie returned to his cell an angry, distraught man. "O God," he blurted in perhaps the first prayer of his life, "if you'll get me out of this hellhole, I promise I'll serve you for the rest of my life." He didn't fully comprehend what he had just said; he only knew he was on a track to nowhere and nothing.

A year later, without warning, Fernando Aranda's name was called at two o'clock in the morning for release. This had to be a mistake, he told himself. He had served only thirteen years of his sentence. Maybe they were going to drive him out into the desert and just shoot him. But when he stepped onto the Greyhound bus at the terminal a few hours later, with clean clothes and some money in his pocket, he really did recognize that he was free.

That evening he got off the bus in El Monte, California, his old neighborhood. "It's amazing how Satan sets things up for you," he recalls. Right there *at the depot* was a guy named Robert whom he hadn't seen in more than a decade. Immediately Robert ushered him toward a nearby motel, where every allurement from drugs to girls was waiting. A three-day binge followed.

> A man came up to him and said, with no introduction, "Hey, guess what? Jesus loves you." Fernie was repulsed.

That Saturday morning, Robert and Fernie headed out toward the beach to meet a contact for more drugs. Suddenly Robert hissed, "Look out! There's the Drug Task Force!" Fernie handed off his cash and prison ID to Robert and raced toward a nearby park, where a crowd of people had gathered for some music. He quickly blended into the group.

Soon a man came up to him and said, with no introduction, "Hey, guess what? Jesus loves you."

Fernie was repulsed. He immediately turned to leave. But as he did, he glimpsed the police coming toward him. He decided his best option was to dive back into the crowd—which was actually a street rally sponsored by a group called Victory Outreach Ministries.

What happened next defies prediction. As Fernie tells it: "I'd never seen any of these people in my life. But a young man named Louie approached me next. He looked sort of like the Marlboro Man—big muscles, big mustache. He walked up to me and boldly said, 'Hey, bro—don't you remember the day you prayed in your prison cell, that if God would release you from that hellhole, you'd serve him the rest of your life?'

"I couldn't believe it! I was stunned. How could this man know anything about my prayer more than a year before?

"I suddenly felt I was no longer hearing the voice of a man. It was the voice of God."

Before Fernie could reply, the man pointed a finger right between his eyes and said, "And you know what you have to do."

This was enough to make Fernando Aranda crumble to his knees there on the grass. He began to weep. "God, I'm sorry! Forgive me of all my sins." The power of God was driving this tough criminal to the point of full surrender.

The next thing Fernie remembers is a small, sweet female voice saying, "Let's take him home!" He looked up to see a girl named Georgina, the daughter of Pastor Sonny Arguinzoni, who heads up Victory Outreach Ministries.

"Yes! Take me home. Please!" he whimpered.

Within minutes the ministry team had put him in a car and headed in the direction of his mother's house. But then, about a mile away, they stopped instead at Victory's group home for men, where more than fifty guys were being discipled toward a new walk with Christ.

Fernie's mother eventually came to see him there. Her prior glimpse of him in prison shackles turned out not to be her final view after all. She saw her son being revolutionized by the cleansing power of the blood of Christ. After three years of intense training, Fernie began to appear in crusades, churches, and other outreaches, telling his amazing story.

When he speaks these days, he sometimes finishes with the driving gospel song made famous by Johnny Cash, "My God Is Real." Audiences (including those at the Brooklyn Tabernacle) weep as he belts out the message:

> ... He's real in my soul!
> My God is real, for he has washed and made me whole!
> His love for me is like pure gold,
> My God is real, and I can feel him in my soul![5]

The blood of the Lamb of God is strong enough to break the chains of drugs and crime. It overwhelms bad habits, bad socioeconomics, and bad friendships. It is the Passover to fulfill all Passover meals, freeing us from the punishments we deserve. It is the center of our hope and faith in Christ. It is God's provision for all the messes we find ourselves in.

When we anchor ourselves in the three lessons of Gilgal — praise for all his past blessings, a sincere heart that repents of sin, and full faith in the work of Christ on the cross — we are then squarely in the place where God can bless us. We are ready to enter into "more."

THE
FORGOTTEN ONE

On a cold and blustery Saturday in January 1969, some 200 people gathered for a six o'clock wedding at a modest church in the Bay Ridge section of Brooklyn. To the west, the winter sun had already sunk behind the towers and cables of the new Verrazano-Narrows Bridge, increasing the chill in the air. Inside the sanctuary, however, the lights were on and the beautiful arrangements of white calla lilies were in place for a festive occasion.

The twenty-six-year-old groom, who worked in midtown Manhattan as a personnel representative, waited nervously at the front for his beautiful bride to enter. She, a receptionist for a large pharmaceutical firm in the city, was resplendent in her white, Spanish-style wedding gown, with a long train descending from the tiara atop her head. The couple truly loved the Lord and had been praying for his presence at their special occasion. They wanted this day to be remembered not just for its smooth ceremony and joyous reception, but also for the touch of God upon all that occurred.

The forty-minute ceremony came to its peak when the middle-aged minister announced at last, "And now you may kiss the bride." The recessional followed, then a receiving line, then photography, and finally the reception. The bride's parents had arranged for a delicious catered dinner to be served in the church's fellowship hall. Guests sat at nicely decorated tables.

When the father of the bride, a minister himself as well as a talented vocalist, arose to address the crowd, he did not propose a toast or engage in humorous remarks. Instead, he made a few introductory comments and then offered up a gospel song of that era, accompanied by a pianist. It seemed almost a prayer for the young couple to adopt as their own:

> Fill my cup, Lord, I lift it up, Lord!
> Come and quench this thirsting of my soul;
> Bread of heaven, feed me till I want no more—
> Fill my cup, fill it up, and make me whole.[1]

An atmosphere of worship came over the assembled guests. Some closed their eyes in reverence, some nodded their heads, others set down their coffee cups and gently raised their hands in praise. A murmur of prayer and adoration spread across the hall when the song finished. The mood turned from party-like to praiseful. People interceded for God to bless these newlyweds and fill their life together with the richness of his Spirit.

No one was in a hurry to break the flow of what had sprung up spontaneously. The bride and groom sat quietly, their heads bowed in prayer. And then, unexpectedly, a woman in her mid-thirties came out of the crowd and stepped up before them. She began to speak.

At first she prayed a blessing for the couple, but soon her words changed to a prophetic declaration, the kind of thing one might have heard in Bible times. She spoke from no prepared script at all. Her inspiration instead seemed to come in the present moment as she said, "… The hand of the Lord is upon you both; God has chosen you for his special work. He will use you in ways you could never imagine. The day will come when you will stand before thousands and thousands of people, speaking the message of God. Your influence will go well beyond anything your mind can fathom on this day. You will travel around the world telling people of the love and grace of Jesus Christ."

> The woman's words carried a ring of authority, yet they were delivered in tenderness.

The woman's words carried a ring of authority, yet they were delivered in tenderness. She concluded with a statement that God's favor would rest upon the wedding couple as they faithfully surrendered to his leading. When she stopped, a fresh swell of praise to God rose up from the guests, while both the bride and groom found themselves in tears. It was several minutes before they regained their composure.

On the plane to Hawaii the next afternoon, the young man mulled in his mind, "What was that all about? It doesn't make any sense. We both have our jobs in the business world; we don't have any training for ministry; we haven't even discussed that kind of life. How could those things ever happen?" When he talked with his new wife about it a few days later, neither one could solve the puzzle.

Who Are We Missing?

I am fully aware that some might dismiss such an event as religious fanaticism or an emotional imitation of phenomena that ended with the apostolic age. But I can vouch for the truth of this story because I was the groom that day and Carol was the bride. I can also tell you that every word the woman spoke that day has literally come to pass. We have not sought to fulfill her prophecy; in fact, in the early days we fought against such a turn in our careers. However, in looking over what God has brought to pass in our years of ministry, I can only conclude that his Spirit wanted to say something important that wedding day, and he chose an inconspicuous but willing person to serve as his messenger. She was no less—or more—than Ananias of Damascus, whom the Lord sent to find Saul in his blindness and tell him amazing things about his future (see Acts 9). She was another in the line of Philip the evangelist's "four unmarried daughters who prophesied" (Acts 21:9).

More significantly, I am convinced that more of these moments would happen in all of our lives if we paid more attention to the person I sometimes refer to as the Forgotten One. Christians generally respect the person of the Holy Spirit, of course, but most of us do not think about him very much. We plan our futures and pursue our goals with the hope that God will bless all that we do. But very few are conscious of the living, active Spirit of God who waits to take his rightful place in our lives.

> Joshua had assumed he was the senior commander. So who was this fellow who showed up unannounced and holding a sword?

This kind of thinking has been a problem for God's people all through history. It was a similar problem that nearly tripped up Joshua. The Bible tells us, "Now when Joshua was near Jericho, he looked up and saw a man standing in front of him with a drawn sword in his hand. Joshua went up to him and asked, 'Are you for us or for our enemies?'" (Josh. 5:13).

Joshua had assumed he was the senior commander on the ground. Moses was gone; he was in charge. He had already identified Jericho, on the horizon, as Target Number One. He was now preparing to launch his first major offensive in the Promised Land. He was probably nervous and certainly prayerful as he waited for the battle to begin.

So who was this fellow who showed up unannounced and holding a sword? What was he doing here? Whose regiment did he belong to?

"Friend or foe?!" Joshua barked.

Isn't it amazing that Joshua appeared almost ready to *fight* the Visitor who was in fact his key to victory? We often do the same foolish thing today. God shows up in the middle of our situation, and we nervously question his identity rather than discerning his powerful presence.

The rest of the biblical account is well-known. The Forgotten One answered Joshua's question directly:

> "Neither," he replied, "but as commander of the army of the LORD I have now come." Then Joshua fell face-down to the ground in reverence, and asked him, "What message does my Lord have for his servant?"
>
> The commander of the LORD's army replied, "Take off your sandals, for the place where you are standing is holy." And Joshua did so (Josh. 5:14–15).

The Bible does not give us any extra identification for this "commander of the Lord's army"—whether he was the pre-incarnate Jesus or the Lord God in a special manifestation. We do not know, and probably do not need to know. What is much more significant for us is to recognize that this heavenly personage was *seriously underestimated* and *almost overlooked*. Joshua had no idea in the beginning who was confronting him. He didn't think this person was important at all. He didn't realize how much he needed the Visitor's help. He soon learned better.

Not Just a "Ghost"

Christians today are generally reverent toward God the Father, and we give well-deserved praise to his Son, our Savior. The member of the Trinity who most often gets neglected in our songs, prayers, and preaching is the Holy Spirit. He is not some amorphous liquid or gas; he is a real person, co-eternal with the Father and the Son. He was in the beginning with them both; in fact, Genesis 1:2 specifically states that "the Spirit of God was hovering over the waters" at the start of creation.

Those of us who grew up with the King James Version of the Bible read often about the "Holy Ghost," and maybe that is part of our problem. As a child, I found the term a bit spooky. I had no desire to get to know a ghost, holy or otherwise.

But in fact, Bible translations have long since removed this obstruction by switching to "Holy Spirit," and he is not some scary specter. He is a person whom all believers should want to know and follow. He is a living being who has feelings and speaks to God's people. We find this mentioned repeatedly in the New Testament. It was an accepted fact that after Jesus ascended, he sent the Holy Spirit to take his place among the disciples. Just as our Lord promised, the Spirit began his vital ministry in the early church, as expressed in the New Testament:

> While they were worshiping the Lord and fasting, *the Holy Spirit said*, "Set apart for me Barnabas and Saul for the work to which I have called them" (Acts 13:2).
>
> *The Spirit clearly says* that in later times some will abandon the faith and follow deceiving spirits and things taught by demons (1 Tim. 4:1).

So, *as the Holy Spirit says:* "Today, if you hear his voice, do not harden your hearts as you did in the rebellion ..." (Heb. 3:7–8).

"Whoever has ears, let them hear *what the Spirit says* to the churches" (Rev. 2:7 and following).

We need to pay close attention to the Spirit's words, the way the Antioch church did, as mentioned above. The minute the Spirit singled out Barnabas and Saul for ministry, the group didn't just move along to the next item on a pre-established order of service. They "fasted and prayed, [then] placed their hands on them and sent them off" to preach the gospel in new territories (Acts 13:3).

This is one of the vital things the Holy Spirit does: he directs individuals into kingdom work. He makes things happen for the advancement of the Father's purposes. He equips ordinary men and women to do extraordinary things. If we don't believe this and become insensitive to the voice of the Spirit, we will miss wonderful things that God has planned for us. We will stay bound to mere facts and theories about the Lord without ever experiencing the power of God in our lives and circumstances.

The Spirit was active in the Old Testament as well. We will highlight just four of many occasions in the book of Judges when the Spirit launched people into doing exploits for God.

Othniel

The first person is Othniel, nephew of the famous Caleb, who was one of the twelve spies sent to scope out Canaan before the Israelite invasion. "The Spirit of the LORD came on him, so that he became Israel's judge [or 'leader'] and went to war. The LORD gave [the] king of Aram into the hands of Othniel, who overpowered him. So the land had peace for forty years, until Othniel son of Kenaz died" (Judg. 3:10–11).

This military achievement was no small feat. The Israelites had been bullied and pushed around by this neighboring king for quite a while. Othniel rose up and turned the tide—for forty years. Imagine any political leader today who handled his job so well that his country stayed out of costly conflict for the next four decades. He would be a national hero. Schoolchildren would end up writing stories about him. His face would no doubt be engraved on a main coin or currency bill. That is what Othniel achieved—because "the Spirit of the LORD came on him."

Gideon

The second person to notice in Judges is the shy, timid, self-deprecating Gideon. He grew up convinced he was nobody. He seemed destined to be a classic example of the underachiever. He expected nothing of himself, or anyone else in his family for that matter. When an angel showed up one day and called him a "mighty warrior" who would throw out the Midianite oppressors, he replied with half a dozen excuses and apologies. He could never do anything significant, he told the visitor.

Yet, as time went on, Gideon found out otherwise. The moment finally arrived when "the Spirit of the LORD came on Gideon, and he blew a trumpet, summoning the Abiezrites [his clan] to follow him. He sent messengers throughout Manasseh, calling them to arms, and also into Asher, Zebulun and Naphtali, so that they too went up to meet them" (Judg. 6:34–35). Who, Gideon? He had never taken charge of anything in his life. But now the Holy Spirit was empowering him, and within two days an incredible victory unfolded for Israel.

Jephthah

The third leader is the little-known Jephthah. It wasn't his fault, of course, that he was born as the result of his father visiting a prostitute. His half-brothers scorned him and let him know he didn't fit with the rest of the family. They bumped him out eventually, and he gathered "a gang of scoundrels" to be his posse (Judg. 11:3). Through his various comments we get the distinct impression of a man with a chip on his shoulder. He spoke too quickly, without measuring his words.

Yet, when the nation got into trouble and desperately needed a leader, the elders turned to this man. And in that moment, "the Spirit of the LORD came on Jephthah. He crossed Gilead and Manasseh, passed through Mizpah of Gilead, and from there he advanced against the Ammonites.... And the LORD gave them into his hands" (Judg. 11:29, 32). The Spirit's anointing overrode his quirks and human weaknesses.

Samson

Finally, of course there is Samson—set apart from birth to serve God, and given extraordinary physical powers to do so. Yet what Samson achieved on Israel's behalf was more than just a matter of bulging biceps. *Four times* the Scripture says something else about him:

The Spirit of the LORD began to stir him ... (Judg. 13:25).

The Spirit of the LORD came on him in power so that he tore the lion apart with his bare hands (Judg. 14:6).

Then the Spirit of the LORD came on him in power. He went down to Ashkelon [and] struck down thirty of their men (Judg. 14:19).

The Spirit of the LORD came on him in power. The ropes on his arms became like charred flax, and the bindings dropped from his hands. Finding a fresh jawbone of a donkey, he grabbed it and struck down a thousand men (Judg. 15:14–15).

Yes, Samson (like Jephthah,[2] and even Gideon[3]) embarrassed himself later in life through an unwise choice. But that does not negate the fact that God used these men in powerful ways to accomplish divine goals. And all they achieved was through the enabling of the Holy Spirit.

The same Holy Spirit is the one who empowers us today to do great things for God—imperfect though we be. He takes us with all our limitations and raises us up to handle challenges that otherwise scare us. He makes the critical difference in our work for the Lord.

"Let the Holy Ghost Work"

D. L. Moody, the great evangelist of the late nineteenth century, once said in a sermon preached here in New York, "We want the Holy Ghost to work in our way, and if He doesn't come in that way, we think sometimes it is not the work of God because it has not come in the usual way.... What we [need] to do is to let the Holy Ghost work in His own way."[4]

When anything happens on earth by God's grace, the

Holy Spirit is the divine agent. If a preacher is effective, it is because the Holy Spirit is working. If any of us are encouraged while reading the Bible, it is because of him who is both the author and revealer of Scripture. If someone is convicted of sin, it's because the Holy Spirit has applied heavenly pressure to that person's soul. If someone is comforted in the midst of distress, it is because, in the words of the old song, "the Comforter has come."

A few years ago, an attractive, early-thirties, blonde Australian named Vanessa Holland showed up in our service at the Brooklyn Tabernacle, brought by someone she met in a martial-arts class. She left early that first Sunday to get to her job. The next week, however, she came back alone and stayed for the entire service.

When I invited people to put their trust in Christ that day at the close of my message, she was one of the first to step forward. In fact, she says now with a laugh, "I was so moved that I was basically knocking people over to get to the front. I had never heard anything like this before, that God could forgive me and wipe clean my awful past. It was so real, so right, so true!"

> When anything happens on earth by God's grace, the Holy Spirit is the divine agent.

Vanessa is hardly what you would call gullible or naïve. Before she arrived on our doorstep, she had traveled the world in search of fulfillment. She had tried everything from drugs and sex to self-help cults to astrology to Buddhism. Her mother, whom we later got to know during a visit to the church, openly stated, "We Australians are very laid back. That's why we took to the hippie life back in the sixties and seventies. We don't like rules. We loved the thing about 'freedom'—sex, drugs, and rock 'n' roll. That's how Vanessa and her brothers were brought up; I admit it."

Vanessa remembers as a little girl wandering through adult parties in her home and witnessing all kinds of things a child should never see. As soon as she reached her teenage years, she moved in with a boyfriend and began imitating the lifestyle of her parents. "There would always be a bunch of guys hanging around our apartment drinking and smoking pot," she says. "I started getting really depressed about this time. So at seventeen, I moved to the other side of Australia and hung out with a crowd much older than me. I thought it was cool ... but at the same time, I felt like I didn't really belong."

By nineteen Vanessa and a girlfriend had saved up enough money to attempt a trip around the world. First stop: New York. Vanessa absolutely fell in love with the city. "It was so alive; it had so much to distract me from my growing unhappiness." She decided to stay here. She found a boyfriend who could support her through selling drugs, robbing people, and running credit card scams.

The next dozen years were a sad series of escapades of looking for peace in all the wrong places: New Age books and seminars, "body work" (treatments from self-appointed healers who wave their hands over you in an attempt to "straighten out your chakras"), charting her astrological markers, and of course, relationships with men. "But I somehow dated only thugs!" Vanessa now says with regret. "I got in the most dreadful situations you can imagine, each one worse than the one before." She tried to make better decisions based on a small bag of divination stones with little markings. They failed to lead her where she should go.

At one point Vanessa linked up with a group of friends to form a "family—three gay men and three of us girls. Maybe this would make me feel better and lift my depression." Soon, however, one girl became a heroin addict. One of the men developed AIDS and got terribly sick. A couple of the others moved away.

On the phone to Australia, Vanessa would moan, "Mum, why did you even have to bring me into this world? There's just no point to my life." She developed more than one suicide plan and looked forward to pulling them off, but never did.

On the phone to Australia, Vanessa would moan, "Mum, why did you even have to bring me into this world? There's just no point to my life."

Then the woman in the martial-arts class mentioned her church. "Sure, why not?" Vanessa replied. "I've tried everything else. I've got nothing to lose." She knew virtually nothing about Christianity. It had some connection to Christmas, she vaguely assumed, but beyond that she drew a total blank.

The instant she walked into the building and sat down, she sensed something very different. Soon the choir began to sing. "I didn't know what was going on, but I started to cry," Vanessa recalls. "That really was not like me, because I had become very hard.

"I had been in large audiences before, listening to New Age lecturers—but I'd always felt very alone there. This was absolutely the opposite. I felt warm and safe in this place. I didn't know it at the time, but it was the Holy Spirit just enveloping me."

That first visit was cut short because of work, but a week later she returned, listened to the full message, and then raced to the front in tears to give her heart to the Lord. "Pastor Cymbala talked about being forgiven of your sins that day. I wanted that *so badly*. I wanted all the junk of my past to be swept away. I wanted to get rid of the anger and depression. I was so hungry for relief from the pain of living the way I'd been living all my life."

The Spirit of God had broken through this young woman's many facades to bring her home at last.

"The change in my life was so real, and so immediate, that it shocked me," she says. "Nothing had ever changed me for more than five minutes before. Now, all of a sudden, I was joyful and excited about life. I also felt offended by my old actions.

"I was managing a restaurant—a big achievement, I had told myself, even though I had gotten the job only because I was sleeping with the owner. Among the staff there, I was known for my absolutely filthy mouth. It was kind of my Aussie thing; we make an art form out of vulgarity, it seems. Whenever anything went wrong, the cooks and waiters were almost entertained by this chick cutting loose with a torrent of nasty language in a Down Under accent.

"Well, that very week after I went to the altar at the Brooklyn Tabernacle, something happened at work, and I blurted out a vulgar word. Instantly I was mortified! I actually gasped and clutched my throat in reaction. What had been commonplace in my life now became a knife in my heart. I was so embarrassed!"

Other changes began to sprout. "Suddenly I realized I was no longer afraid of the dark, which is something I'd always suffered. My roommate used to tease me about having every light in the place on at five in the morning. I think it traced back to weird things in my childhood, playing the Ouija board with my mum when I was little, and all that.

"Anyway, now the problem vanished. I could turn out the lights when I went to bed and feel nothing but coziness. Darkness no longer triggered my apprehension."

Today Vanessa Holland runs her own business as a personal trainer, assisted by two part-time employees. Her life has stabilized, and her outlook is positive. She found out along the way that her mother had come to the Lord just as dramatically back in Australia and had been fervently praying for her daughter to find peace on the other side of the globe. To see them worshiping together in our church when her mother came to visit moved me deeply. While she was here, in fact, we videotaped them both for a clip that appears on the choir's 2006 DVD, *I'm Amazed ... LIVE*. The clip includes photos from her unruly past as well as her riveting testimony.

Her summary Scripture these days, Vanessa says, is Romans 15:13, which talks about how "the God of hope [can] fill you will all joy and peace as you trust in him, so that you may overflow with hope *by the power of the Holy Spirit*." The major cleansing of her life has been nothing short of a work of the Spirit of God.

The Spirit of Holiness

We didn't program Vanessa to clean up her act. We didn't say she had to stop swearing, doing drugs, or sleeping around. The Holy Spirit took care of all that from the inside out. It was a case of what the Lord said through the prophet Ezekiel long before Jesus came: "I will give you a new heart and put a new spirit in you; I will remove from you your heart of stone and give you a heart of flesh. And I will put my Spirit in you and *move you to follow my decrees* and be careful to keep my laws" (Ezek. 36:26–27). The Spirit of God was the motivating, activating force inside her soul.

Who among us can live in purity by willpower alone? Yet Jesus calls us to personal holiness. He is serious about this requirement, no doubt; he is not just spinning idle words. He expects us to be holy as he is holy. And the One who calls us will also equip us.

One of the New Testament's most straightforward paragraphs says at the end, "God did not call us to be impure, but to live a holy life. Therefore, anyone who rejects this instruction does not reject a human being but God, the very God *who gives you his Holy Spirit*" (1 Thess. 4:7–8).

If the Holy Spirit remains the Forgotten One in our spiritual walk, we will fail to become the pure and joyful person God planned for us to be. We simply won't succeed. There is no holy living outside of the Holy Spirit's control. That, in fact, is part of his name; he is called the *Holy* Spirit for good reason.

He works deep inside us to change our desires from pleasing ourselves to pleasing God. He also uses the Word of God to enable us to control our thought lives. The Holy Spirit is the only one who can subdue the strong urgings of the lower nature. He is the only one who can break habits that have been repeated countless times. He is the only one who can overcome Satan and all his subtle temptations.

The more we walk in the Spirit, the more we share Christ's attitude toward sin. We get beyond simply turning over a new leaf or promising to be different. We start to think about sin the way God does, and we are repulsed by it, just as Vanessa Holland was that day in the restaurant. This too is a work of the Spirit.

One word picture in the Bible for the Holy Spirit is *fire*. John the Baptist foretold that on the day of Pentecost the early Christians would be baptized "with the Holy Spirit and fire" (Matt. 3:11). That, in fact, is what appeared that day as tongues of fire hovered above the 120 disciples. The apostle Paul wrote to one church years later, "Do not put out the Spirit's fire" (1 Thess. 5:19).

Fire has at least three remarkable properties that help us understand the work of the Spirit.

1. *Fire penetrates whatever it touches.* Wood is not the same once it is set on fire. Neither is plastic or carpet—or skin. Fire goes deep below the surface and alters the very molecular structure of whatever it invades.

The Spirit has a way of penetrating to essentials below the surface of our lives. "The Spirit searches all things" (1 Cor. 2:10). If there is brooding resentment against someone or some situation, the Spirit puts his finger on that problem and calls us to forgive. What does not please him becomes the center of his focus. "He will bring to light what is hidden in darkness and will expose the motives of people's hearts" (1 Cor. 4:5).

Spirit-anointed preaching has a way of getting to the heart of matters that are truly important. These sermons are not just clever or entertaining. They dig down to areas that need God's attention. In his memoirs, evangelist Charles G. Finney wrote, "I could not preach unless I went into the woods to seek the Lord so that my words would penetrate the people. I knew when the Spirit was upon me because it made the people uncomfortable."

> The Spirit has a way of penetrating to essentials below the surface of our lives. What does not please him becomes the center of his focus.

When the Spirit helps us to pray, he penetrates deep inside us, enabling us to give expression to the deepest desires of our heart. We don't just say nice-sounding phrases. Some of the most powerful public praying I've ever heard has come from people anointed by the Holy Spirit, whose words were very simple—but everyone knew the words came from their hearts as well as the heart of God. There was no attempt at eloquence or fine-sounding phrases. The prayer instead came from the very bottom of the soul.

The Holy Spirit destroys whatever is flammable. He burns up what doesn't belong in our lives, the "wood, hay or straw" (1 Cor. 3:12) that are going to be exposed on the day of judgment anyway. They might as well get burned out now.

2. Fire serves as a light. It leads us like a lantern. That is how the Israelites got through the trackless desert, of course. A pillar of cloud and a pillar of fire led the way (Exod. 13:21–22).

The Holy Spirit is a bright and shining guide for us. Are we following him, or are we meandering off on our own side trails? If we insist on charting our own path and wind up getting lost, we have no one to blame but ourselves. The fire of the Spirit knows the best course for each of us and lives today to guide us.

As one insightful leader wrote, "If Israel followed this pillar of fire and cloud so carefully, how much more should we follow the Holy Spirit? . . . The organized church has largely proven a tremendous framework of form and ceremony, built up against God himself. The Holy Spirit has no right of way. . . . We have got to leave room for God somewhere."[5]

Doesn't this describe the bland predictability of many of our services today?

3. Fire is contagious. It spreads from one location to the next. Wherever there is willing fuel, it leaps up.

If we are ablaze with God's Spirit, we are bound to affect other people. This is the history of every spiritual awakening, from Jonathan Edwards' day in the 1740s to the noontime prayer meetings just before the Civil War, to the Welsh Revival, to any other movement of God you care to mention. These movements were incendiary. People were touched by the fire of God, and soon the heat spread to others, whose lives were changed as well.

❦

Have you ever noticed the motto emblazoned across the Salvation Army's crest? It reads, "Blood and Fire." Maybe you thought those words simply signified having a courageous spirit to get out on the street and face the difficult needs of humanity—sort of like "blood and guts." No, that is not their meaning at all. General William Booth, the founder, was very specific: "The blood is the blood of Christ, and the fire is the fire of the Holy Ghost."[6] That is what drove the passion and work of the early Salvationists. We need the same blood and fire today.

> If we are ablaze with God's Spirit, it is bound to affect other people. This is the history of every spiritual awakening.

If we don't want this kind of intense passion for the Lord ... if we would rather not be made pure in our daily living ... if we don't want to be led in new and challenging directions ... then our only choice is to keep our distance from the Holy Spirit. Hold him at arm's length. Don't let his heat start to warm our faces. Too many people in too many churches are living just that way today. We forget about the Holy Spirit, even while holding to orthodox doctrine. This neglect of the Forgotten One is probably the greatest cause of spiritual malaise. It is also a human tragedy in light of God's great promises for us.

The only route to our Promised Land is outlined in God's Word, and the one who can empower us and guide us there is God the Holy Spirit. Today is the first day of the rest of all our lives. Whatever the past failures or heartaches, we cannot undo one single day. But we can open our hearts afresh to the Holy Spirit and begin to draw from him all the heavenly resources he supplies.

CHAPTER 5

LESSON FROM THE BAYOU

The prison officer wiped the sweat from his forehead as he gave his crop of new inmates a blunt piece of advice. "There are not enough of us guards to protect you guys here," he admitted. "So find someone to make you a knife. If someone tries to hurt you or take advantage of you — you know what I mean — kill him as fast as you can. Chances are no one will ever inform on you, and you'll establish respect so you don't get messed with again."

Standing nearby was a seasoned inmate who nodded his head. The newcomers could not help noticing, however, that the inmate openly carried a weapon. He had been deputized as a guard to help control his fellow prisoners, even though he was as guilty of serious crimes as they. In the minds of the prison bosses, this was all part of normal operations — plus it saved money by not having to hire so many legitimate correctional staff.

This was a sprawling maximum-security complex along the banks of a winding river, with more than 5,000 inmates. Most had arrived with a no-parole life sentence, meaning they would spend the rest of their days here in the single-story, cinder block buildings that ranged across the flat, humid landscape. Those days might easily be cut short, however, by the flash of a knife, the blast of a rifle, or even the flick of a cigarette lighter. "The guards would pay an inmate to take care of anyone they didn't like," one man recalls. "They'd allow the guy to run into your cell and stab you or set you on fire. The men kept buckets of water under their beds so if someone had gasoline or lighter fluid, they could put out the fire if they got burned." Hence, the media were not exaggerating by calling this "America's bloodiest prison."

When an inmate finally died, he often had outlived any family members who still cared to arrange for a proper funeral. So he was buried inside the walls, surrounded even in death by barbed wire. The prison management—again, to save money—bought the cheapest caskets they could find on the market, made of cardboard. One rainy afternoon, the ultimate indignity occurred when the soggy bottom fell out of a casket just as it was being lifted into place at the open grave. Fellow inmate mourners gasped as the dead body tumbled into the hole. A guard simply motioned for the workmen to dump the rest of the casket onto the body and then proceed to shovel the dirt back into place, covering up the whole mess as quickly as possible.

In contrast, I well remember the visit Carol and I made with the Brooklyn Tabernacle Singers in 2005 to a prison that could not have been more different. Guards carried no weapons at all, not even nightsticks. Inmates belonged to some thirty different clubs that encouraged everything from public speaking to hobbies. Education classes were in full swing. One group of inmates was repairing and refurbishing 160 broken wheelchairs a month as part of Joni Eareckson Tada's "Wheels for the World" program, providing free mobility to the disabled in foreign countries.

Five different congregations worshiped together, and not just on Sunday mornings. Weeknight services were common, attended by large crowds of men. Inmate bands led the music, and even the preaching was often done by inmates who had received training through a nearby seminary that brought its classes and full degree programs to the penitentiary. Baptisms were frequent; more than a thousand men were said to be devout Christians. Some of the worship and preaching teams were even allowed to travel to outside bookings, ministering in churches and conferences across the state. They were accompanied by only a single guard, unarmed.

I was often amazed at the spiritual depth of some of the men I spoke to. They may have been serving a double life sentence plus ninety-nine extra years, but their eyes were filled with purpose and joy. In the meetings, the surge of praise and prayer from hundreds of voices lifted together was genuine. I felt it a high privilege to be among them.

One Man's Crusade

Now here is the surprise: *Both of these accounts describe the same prison.* I am speaking of the 18,000-acre Louisiana State Penitentiary sixty miles northwest of Baton Rouge, commonly known as "Angola." It has a well-documented history of abuse and brutality. Food and medical treatment in the late 1800s were hardly enough to keep the inmates alive. Many died at the hands of fellow prisoners. Those who were put to work building levees to control the Mississippi River knew that any inmate who died would simply be dropped into the growing mounds of dirt. After all, it would save the trouble of hauling wheelbarrows of extra dirt.

So what happened to change the culture of this dreadful place?

A short, silver-haired warden named Burl Cain arrived in early 1995. His predecessor had told him he would last no more than five years. Another person claimed there were demons over the place. Cain's response? "I'm going to run them off, with God's help."

Burl Cain established from the first day that he would treat inmates with respect. He shocked some by sitting down to eat with them in the dining hall. There he was appalled at the poor quality of food and quickly ordered the kitchen staff to do better. It did not matter to him whether the prisoners were white, like him, or of some other race. He became a walking demonstration of the Golden Rule: "Do to others what you would have them do to you" (Matt. 7:12). He put himself in the place of one who had made a big mistake in life and been sentenced to Angola. How would he want to be treated? As a human being, or a dangerous animal?

Cain began training his staff to stop the insults and name-calling. He opened up new opportunities for study and achievement. He threw his full efforts behind the annual rodeo, where inmates got to perform for the visiting public and also to sell crafts made throughout the year. An arena seating 9,000 was built (with private money); each October it is packed out for the festivities.

But this warden is no soft touch. He knows how to crack down hard—but with fairness—on infractions. He has proved to all concerned that it's not wise to challenge him.

He calls his strategy "moral rehabilitation," by which he means learning to live peacefully and productively in a prison community. "I realized I could teach them to read and write, could help them learn skills and a trade," Cain says, "but without moral rehabilitation, I would only be creating a smarter criminal." That is why his emphasis on spiritual growth has been given such priority. Angola is a place where increasing numbers of prisoners *want* to do the right thing before God.

As a result, you can walk around the institution and hardly believe you are in a penitentiary. Large numbers of men live not in cells but in open dormitories. They greet their chief with "How ya doin', Warden Cain? Praise the Lord!" They know him as a man who looks for ways to say yes to their requests, rather than always saying no.

The average sentence length at Angola is still eighty-eight years, given this population of murderers, rapists, and repeat violent felons. The tough Louisiana laws and policies are still as tight as ever against granting parole, even to well-behaved prisoners; it seldom happens. Yet hope is alive in this place. The annual capture of contraband weapons each year is down from nearly 800 in the past to fewer than 50 last year.

> Warden Cain established from the first day that he would treat inmates with respect. He shocked some by sitting down to eat with them in the dining hall.

When a man on Death Row has finished all the legal procedures and comes to the day of execution, he is accompanied every step of the way by Burl Cain. The warden attends the prisoner's final meal and eats with him. He spends hours answering the convicted man's questions, explaining in detail how lethal injection works, going over every step of the coming hours. He then prays with the inmate.

On the way to the death chamber is a reception area with two large murals painted by prisoners. One depicts Elijah in a fiery chariot rising to heaven; the other shows Daniel standing fearlessly in the lion's den. When the fateful hour comes, Burl Cain is present at the gurney. He takes the man's hand, looks into his eyes, and gently offers words of comfort. Only then does he do what the state requires of him: he nods to the executioner to start the flow of toxic drugs into the man's veins.

A few minutes later, Cain stands before the waiting media to make his trademark announcement: "We have now sent [name] to his final judgment." He deliberately avoids using the words *execution* or *death*.

For any funeral on penitentiary grounds, the scene could not be more opposite from the old days of cardboard caskets. The prison's woodworking shop builds exquisite oak coffins, hand-polished to perfection. (They are so impressive that Samaritan's Purse president Franklin Graham bought two of them for the use of his famous parents, Billy and Ruth Graham.) On funeral day, the casket is reverently loaded onto a black antique hearse wagon with glass sides, pulled by two massive Percheron horses. The inmate driver sits high above, wearing a tuxedo with a black top hat.

The procession moves slowly toward the prison's Point Lookout Cemetery. There, whitewashed cement crosses mark each grave. To the very end, those whom society has locked away are treated with dignity and respect. As one of his assistants puts it, "It's one thing to say that inmates are human. It's another to treat them that way. The warden has taught me how to do that."[1]

Beyond Categories

When we look at people the way God looks at them, we see value and potential. We go beyond the details of skin color, language, gender, and age to the point of loving the person God created. He would not have given this person divine breath if he had no purpose for their life. He meant for them to be appreciated and developed.

Of all the mottos Burl Cain could have adopted to bring about a revolution at Angola, he could not have chosen a better one than the Golden Rule:

"Do to others what you would have them do to you."

This simple eleven-word sentence did not just show up in a collection of random sayings somewhere. No less than the Son of God authored it—and he said it "sums up the Law and the Prophets" (Matt. 7:12). What an amazing claim!

If you have read the Old Testament, you know that it is lengthy (883 pages in my Bible), complex, and even confusing in places. Some of its laws seem terribly irrelevant. For example, what is so bad about wearing clothes woven of two different materials (Lev. 19:19)? Most of us do it all the time and cannot imagine why we shouldn't. Some Christians have stopped reading the Old Testament altogether (except possibly the book of Psalms). Others, however, have gotten tangled up trying to apply Old Testament practices to New Testament Christianity, trying to "claim the blessings of Abraham" or "restore the tabernacle of David." They ignore the wise guideline that says if

> When we look at people the way God looks at them, we go beyond the details of skin color, language, gender, and age.

a law or principle goes without reinforcement in the New Testament, it can safely be dismissed. Only the truths repeated under the New Covenant—such as those forbidding murder, adultery, lying, and profanity, to list just a few—are binding upon us as Christian believers. We live in a different age; we breathe different air.

But we cannot shelve the Old Testament entirely. Jesus

certainly didn't. He came to fulfill the law, in fact. And in a stroke of absolute genius he said, in his Sermon on the Mount, that he could boil down the 883 pages to just one sentence. He could sweep all of "the Law and the Prophets" into a single, compelling directive that would revolutionize society. He could summarize all of Exodus, Leviticus, Deuteronomy, and the rest in this brilliant guideline.

To please God, we do not have to spend years in theological training. Neither do we have to master some thick rule book that covers each and every situation. What we have to do is remember, every moment of every day, to treat others as we would like to be treated. As the apostle Paul put it, "Love is the fulfillment of the law" (Rom. 13:10). Love is at the core of what a godly life requires.

If we Christians would, through the grace of God, conscientiously obey this one sentence, we would have covered the essence of God's desire for us. What a difference this would make! It would help us grasp that God's greater blessing for each of us is built on a foundation of selfless love. As Jesus said in his sermon, "You have heard that it was said, 'Love your neighbor and hate your enemy.' But I tell you, love your enemies and pray for those who persecute you, that you may be children of your Father in heaven" (Matt. 5:43–45).

Apparently that love is meant for all kinds of folks—not just "our kind." In fact, God's greater future for you and me is quite likely to involve our association with those who are "other" than we are. God did not promise to pour out his goodness or give his gifts just to white males who speak English, like me. For me to realize God's best in my life entails being open and sensitive to the wide variety of his creation, which I am commanded to treat as honorably as I would want to be treated.

The Israelites' journey to the Promised Land gives us an outstanding example of this truth.

Who would have expected that God's strategic plan for the takeover of Jericho would have included a female Canaanite in a less-than-respectable line of work? Her name was Rahab. The two spies Joshua sent to check out the city and identify its weak points opted to stay at her house. This was part of their camouflage, a way to avoid detection by the Jericho police force.

It didn't work, of course. The king of the city found out soon enough. He sent his officers to investigate, and Rahab deliberately threw them off the trail. This woman, who had been used and abused by men throughout her life, apparently felt no loyalty to help the city fathers now. Instead, she sided with the people of God. "I know that the LORD has given this land to you," Rahab said to the two spies. "... Now then, please swear to me by the LORD that you will show kindness to my family ... and that you will save us from death" (Josh. 2:9, 12–13). The men readily agreed, arranging a signal (a scarlet cord in a window) that would help identify her home during the chaos of battle.

If you have ever taught this story to children in a Sunday school class, you have probably avoided mentioning what Rahab did for a living. She was, in one sense, not exactly an upright and honorable citizen. Yet the New Testament speaks glowingly about her legacy—twice. It includes her in the Faith Hall of Fame in Hebrews 11: "By faith the prostitute Rahab, because she welcomed the spies, was not killed with those who were disobedient" (v. 31). She is praised for the attitude of her heart, which identified with God's people.

The apostle James brings up her name and salutes her bold action: "Was not even Rahab the prostitute considered righteous for what she did when she gave lodging to the spies and sent them off in a different direction? As the body without the spirit is dead, so faith without deeds is dead" (James 2:25–26).

God sometimes has a role to play for those whom we wouldn't choose. He is the master organizer, pulling together talents and personalities from a wide assortment of humanity. They don't all wear the same uniform. They don't all come from the same heritage. Yet the Lord knows what he is doing, and it is not wise for us to second-guess his personnel selections. If he decides to weave people such as Rahab into his plan for deliverance and expansion, our job is simply to remember the Golden Rule and go along with God's plan.

> God sometimes has a role to play for those whom we wouldn't choose.

Another woman whom God used greatly, even in the midst of this male-dominated era, was the judge Deborah. A hundred years or so after the conquest of Canaan, Israel was under the thumb of a cruel king with the latest technology ("nine hundred chariots fitted with iron," Judg. 4:3) and suffered for twenty years. God intervened at last by raising up Deborah. The Bible says she was a prophet, was a well-respected judge of people's disputes, and also (unlike Rahab) was married. She recruited an army commander named Barak, who would manage the fight for freedom.

These two examples from the time of Joshua and the judges show us that "God does not show favoritism" (Acts 10:34). If we truly accept the prophecy of Joel—"I will pour out my Spirit on all people. Your sons and daughters will prophesy.... Even on my servants, both men and women, I will pour out my Spirit in those days" (Joel 2:28–29)—then we need to affirm and welcome the ministry of the Deborahs of our time. Thank God that William Booth, founder of the Salvation Army, did not tell his wife Catherine to sit down, keep quiet, and just raise their eight children. Instead, while William preached to the poor in the streets of London, Catherine met with the wealthy and raised funds. She eventually began preaching herself and, by all accounts, was more effective than her husband.

The same is true regarding those from different ethnic groups, income levels, education levels, and age categories. God is in the business of building a global church, and all of us who aspire to help him had better accept that his ways and thoughts are not like ours. He is not going to limit himself to "our kind" alone.

We cannot expect to experience the "more" God has for us if we fail to love those whom God loves.

Can God Bless Racism?

I am convinced that one of the main obstacles to spiritual revival in this country is racial prejudice in churches. It gets hidden, of course, behind smokescreens such as attempting to serve a "target group" with the gospel and therefore increase attendance figures. This, however, is often a subtle way to exclude those whose color or ethnicity is not wanted. Others, by their very choice of location, betray the fact that they are not very interested in folks from the "wrong" side of town.

One staff member of a large and wealthy church told me that his congregation was most generous when offerings were taken for the victims of Hurricane Katrina back in 2005. People gave abundantly to help those who had been flooded out. Busloads of hurting people ended up coming to resettle in this city.

But then the story took a different twist. A number of

> He asked me in all sincerity, "Pastor, why is it that the Yankees are more integrated than the Christian churches in this country?"

the refugees from New Orleans began showing up to attend this church, having heard that the believers there had been stirred to help them. They wanted to show their appreciation. These newcomers were largely African-American. Some of them began to apply for membership — and that's when the true color of people's hearts began to show. Church members started to leave in a steady trickle. Their reason? They were not fond of having to worship with "those kinds of people."

All this happened even as Christians kept singing about *God's* love for the whole world. They needed to review what Thomas à Kempis, a monk best known for his devotional classic *The Imitation of Christ*, wrote back in the fifteenth century: "To place yourself lower than all mankind can do you no harm; but much harm may be done by preferring yourself to one single individual."[2] Whenever we elevate ourselves above any group of God's people, we remove ourselves from the stream of his blessing.

One of Major League Baseball's greatest pitchers occasionally visits the Brooklyn Tabernacle with his lovely wife and has even given his testimony in a service. They have become good friends of ours over the last few years. We have traveled overseas together to spread the gospel. He came from Central America, and one day sitting in my office, he asked me in all sincerity, "Pastor, why is it that the Yankees are more integrated than the Christian churches in this country?" He talked about how in baseball, nobody cares about your complexion or your last name. All that matters is how you play and support your teammates. He wondered why so many Christians don't think the same way, since we serve a God of love.

I didn't have a good answer for him.

I know of one denomination with extremely strict standards of holiness that they insist are based on the Bible. Unfortunately, those standards have not prevented them from creating a sister denomination, with identical doctrines, for black folks. That way, if one of their white churches is ever visited by a black person, they have a ready referral to put to use. They can just send them down the road to their affiliate group.

These people would not be very comfortable with Burl Cain and the brothers at Angola penitentiary, I can assure you. They are blind to the fact that God's plan for his kingdom on earth is not limited to any one group of people. It reaches literally around the globe. When we gather in heaven, "a great multitude that no one could count, from every nation, tribe, people and language, [will be] standing before the throne and in front of the Lamb" (Rev. 7:9). If we are destined to stand shoulder to shoulder on that day, we might as well get used to it now. God help us to mean it when we pray, "Thy will be done on earth as it is in heaven."

Forerunners to Follow

This is not a new or novel concept born out of a desire to be trendy in the twenty-first century. Genuine Christians all through the ages have realized the bigger scope of the family of God. Among those who serve us well as models are the Moravian believers of the 1700s, who left their villages in central Europe (now the Czech Republic) to live out the Golden Rule in faraway places. It was Moravian missionaries, for example, who impressed the young John Wesley on board a ship to America in 1736 with their calmness during a terrible storm. He stayed in touch with their movement over the next few years as he drew ever closer to his own moment of trusting in Christ.

Other missionary movements in subsequent centuries have drawn greater spotlight; however, they all owe a debt to the Moravians. The Moravians' "do unto others" mentality brought thousands to the Savior. Some converts were so filled with the love of Christ that they sold themselves into slavery in order to reach certain slave groups in the Caribbean; it was the only way they could find to connect. In one case, a few Moravians deliberately contracted leprosy so they could work among lepers. Others worked to build Native American settlements, which were later wiped out by American expansionism.

The Moravian reach literally stretched from Greenland to South Africa—from one end of the earth to the other. Although the English Baptist missionary William Carey is often cited today as "the Father of Modern Missions," he would point instead to the Moravians, whose model he often mentioned in his journal. They faithfully exhibited the love of Jesus to many in need, often at great personal sacrifice.

The gospel of Jesus Christ has everything to do with love. God *is* love. That is meant to be our banner, our advertisement to the hurting world. Jesus said that would be the way people would recognize us as his followers (John 13:35). Stop and reflect a minute: Would we like to learn that after we left the room, people began talking negatively about us? Then let's not do it ourselves. Would we like to be discriminated against on the basis of our color or gender? Then don't judge others by those criteria. Do we who are fathers like to see other men ogling our teenage daughters? Then let's not look at other men's daughters that way. Real Christianity can be reduced to the Golden Rule in all aspects of our lives.

The whole point of the well-known 1 Corinthians 13 is

that love is more important than mountain-moving faith, benevolent giving, supernatural utterances in other tongues, or even martyrdom; it is "the greatest" (v. 13). And it is significant that this was written to a church known for its various strengths. "You do not lack any spiritual gift," the apostle wrote (1 Cor. 1:7). He yearned, however, to see them overcome their sectarian competitive attitudes as followers of Paul, of Apollos, of Cephas, and of Christ. He was looking for genuine, wide-ranging love.

One of the greatest spiritual self-deceptions is the idea that we are living close to God even though we care little about the people around us. This simply does not square with 1 John 4:8: "Whoever does not love does not know God, because God is love." We can study the Bible as diligently as the Pharisees did; we can boast in our doctrinal statements; we can raise lots of money and build impressive church campuses. But if we are not loving others, including those who are unlike ourselves, we are ignoring the truth of 1 John 4:20, which says, "If we do not love a fellow believer, whom we have seen, we cannot love God, whom we have not seen." It is as simple as that.

The only measure of our vertical relationship with God is the loving quality of our horizontal relationship with others. We are not truly acquainted with God if we don't love and respect the human beings for whom Christ died. How is it possible to love the Head and be indifferent to his precious Body, which includes believers of every race and background?

A Big Job Ahead

Moving into the promised future God has in mind for us is a very big project indeed. We do it with others who belong to

93

Christ. It requires the energy and gifts of all his people. We do not have the luxury of excluding anyone from the enterprise. Jericho will not be captured without Rahab's contribution. Sisera and his army will not be overthrown without the leadership of Deborah. If we want to see the fullness of God's victory in our lives, we must embrace every brother and sister whom he embraces.

A poignant reminder of this truth came our way in the aftermath of September 11, 2001. The Brooklyn Tabernacle lost four people that day—the most of any congregation in the city, so far as I know. One was a police officer. He had been an undercover drug agent, which is the most dangerous assignment in the NYPD. Then he met a young woman in our church, and eventually they got married.

When their first child was on the way, he surprised her one day by saying, "Honey, I've been thinking about the fact that I'm going to be a father. I need to stop doing such dangerous work. I want to be sure I'm here for this child. Guess what—I've found an opening with the Port Authority instead. I'll be stationed in the World Trade Center, where I'll be safe. No more chasing drug dealers down the back alleys."

His pregnant wife was thrilled, of course.

Then, on that fateful morning, she was working four blocks away ... and when the building went down, she knew instinctively that she had lost her beloved husband. She would bear this child alone.

For his funeral, my wife, Carol, got a hundred fifty or so choir members to take off work and come to sing. Mayor Rudy Giuliani showed up as well. When I gave him an opportunity to address the crowd, he took the microphone and said, "Mr. and Mrs. Stuart, I want you to know you had a great son. He was a hero. Thelma, your husband was a hero.

All of us are concerned for you today and want to help you anyway we can."

He leaned into the pulpit as he continued. "You know, people, I've learned something through all this. Let me see if I can express it to you. When everybody was fleeing that building, and the cops and the firefighters and the EMS people were heading up into it, do you think any of them said, 'I wonder how many blacks are up there for us to save? I wonder what percentage are whites up here? How many Jews are there? Let's see — are these people making $400,000 a year, or $24,000, or — ?'

> We are God's only representatives on the planet and simply cannot take time to pick and choose who needs help. They all need help.

"No, when you're saving lives, they're all precious. And that's how we're supposed to live all the time. How would you want the cops to treat you if you were on the seventy-fifth floor that day? Would you want them to say, 'Excuse me, but I've got the get the bosses out first?' Not exactly.

"I confess I haven't always lived this way. But I'm convinced that God wants us to do it. He wants us to value every human life the way he does."

I sat there thinking, *My goodness, the mayor is preaching a truth that has eluded so many of our churches throughout New York and the country!* He may have stood for other policies that I could not agree with, but on that day, he was right on the mark. The truth of what he said penetrated my heart.

The world you and I live in is falling apart before our eyes. We are God's only representatives on the planet and simply cannot take time to pick and choose who needs help. They *all* need help. They *all* need the love and forgiveness of Jesus Christ. They *all* need to be rescued from the horror of an eternity apart from God. Christ died for each one and wants "everyone to come to repentance" (2 Pet. 3:9). God cares intensely for every one of them.

Only when we share his heart toward people—and follow through with real, tangible actions of love—can we earn his "Well done, good and faithful servant. Enter into the blessings I have reserved for you."

CHAPTER 6

NOT SO FAST!

It is one thing to be attacked head-on by an enemy. It is another to have somebody "play" you, as we say in New York. And in our effort to take the land we believe God has promised us, we are usually more prepared for the first than the second.

Following the Israelite victories at Jericho and Ai, the nearby cities could well imagine themselves getting picked off one by one. Who would be next? They decided to form a coalition. By pooling their military men and resources, they figured they could mount a stronger resistance to Joshua and his army.

Only one town opted out of this approach. "The people of Gibeon ... resorted to a ruse" (Josh. 9:3–4). Instead of joining the neighbors in forming a large strike force, they pulled together their best Oscar-winning actors and fitted them with elaborate props. By the time all the ragged tunics, patched-up sandals, and cracked wineskins had been assembled with dusty, unwashed donkeys, this troupe looked like gold prospectors lost in a desert for two years.

They stumbled convincingly into the Israelite camp at

Gilgal and told Joshua how terribly long and difficult their journey had been. For weeks they had been on the road, they claimed, until now they had little left in their packs that was fit to eat. All they wanted, they said with pathetic eyes downcast, was a treaty of peace with the invading army, so their poor wives and children back home would not have to worry about the rumors spreading along the trade routes to their distant town.

Joshua most likely assumed these men came from a town well beyond the boundaries God had drawn for Israel's possession. So how could it hurt? Why not be a "nice guy"? Give these folks a break, a little peace of mind.…

The Bible records in a fateful sentence, "The Israelites sampled their provisions *but did not inquire of the Lord*" (v. 14).

Three days after the formalities were ratified by all parties, a scout showed up with shocking news: "Guess what, Joshua—these people are basically just over the hill! Their town is in our front yard, right where we're intending to march next." I can imagine the color of embarrassment that began rising up Joshua's neck and face. This anointed leader had been "played" by some cunning performers.

The people quickly let him know what they thought of this blunder. "The whole assembly grumbled against the leaders" (v. 18). They were even more disgusted when they had to go protect the Gibeonites from an attack by the aggravated coalition (Joshua 10). They had to uphold the solemn word their leader had given before almighty God.

Lion or Liar?

In the spiritual conflicts we face, frontal attacks from Satan are easy to understand. The nature of the battle is clear;

nothing is left to subtlety. The enemy tries to overwhelm us through discouragement, or perhaps he uses some friends to drag down our faith. Perhaps there is a faction in our church that is causing division. We see exactly what is happening, and we pray for God to give us courage and strength. The devil is like a roaring lion, says the New Testament (1 Peter 5:8), and we know he must be confronted.

But when the enemy resorts to trickery and deception, we are sometimes slow to recognize him. We often see only what we want to see instead of what is factually true. Our natural senses lead us astray. In these cases we are dealing not with a noisy *lion* but with a sneaky *liar*—in fact, the father of lies, as Jesus called him (John 8:44). Like Joshua, we come up short in the area of spiritual discernment. God knows what we should do, but we aren't sure. As a result of failing to consult with him, we suffer dire consequences.

> When the enemy resorts to deception, we are sometimes slow to recognize him. In these cases we are dealing not with a noisy lion but with a sneaky liar.

Even good people can get off track if they rush ahead without consulting God. When our natural senses do not detect anything amiss and we lean only on our common sense, we can create a disaster. We need to slow down and remember that what *looks* okay is not always okay. Unless we take time to "inquire of the Lord," we won't know until it's too late. We will make decisions that come back to haunt us.

Some may be skeptical of this kind of inquiry and say it's too mystical or emotion-based. "Just go by the Word," they retort. Well, Joshua and his leadership team were entirely familiar with the Torah—the writings of Moses. They knew all about the Ten Commandments. They were fully informed about God's laws. The trouble is, no verse in the Torah specifically said, "Refuse to make a treaty with those who seem to have come from far away." The Scripture would not directly have helped them avoid this particular deception.

The Israelite leaders needed to quiet their hearts before God and seek his counsel for this situation. What loving father would not want to help his precious children avoid the pitfalls of life? Psalm 73:23–24 says, "You hold me by my right hand. You guide me with your counsel, and afterward you will take me into glory." God wants us to turn to him with every difficult or complicated decision we face. This means admitting that our perspective is limited. We don't know what tomorrow holds. We can't see around the bend in the road—but he can.

We need to follow the example of Rebekah, Isaac's wife, who experienced turbulence during a pregnancy when "the babies jostled each other within her." She didn't have the advantage of a modern sonogram, so she had no way of knowing she was carrying twins. Instead, "she said, 'Why is this happening to me?' So she went to inquire of the LORD" (Gen. 25:22). She knew something unusual was going on—but what? The Lord then revealed a great deal about the future of her two sons.

How many times in our lives do we experience a jostling within, a sense that something is not quite right, but we don't know what it is? This is the time to come away and seek the Lord.

Even Jesus did this, on occasion spending full nights in prayer. He was perfect, yet he felt the need to consult with his Father. Incredibly, our track record for decision making is full of past mistakes—yet we neglect to approach God at the very moment when we need his direction most. We need to get away to our heavenly Father and say, "What is this all about? Are you trying to tell me something? Lead me by your Spirit in the path I should go. Show me things I cannot see with my natural eyes."

Prayer was never meant to be just a recitation of our laundry list of needs and desires. For too many of us, prayer has become a monologue rather than a dialogue. When we run out of things to ask for, we stop praying. If we would stay in God's presence a little longer and listen, he would pour out his heart and mind to us. He would tell us invaluable insights into our circumstances. He would counsel us on some family problem or testy relationship at work. He would reveal whether we should say yes or no to a present opportunity. We need his guidance, and the good news is that he is more than willing to give it if we ask in faith.

More Than Once

David, the "man after God's own heart" (see 1 Sam. 13:14; Acts 13:22), was always at his best when he took time to seek the Lord's will on what he should do. Shortly after David became king, the warlike Philistines decided to test his resolve. Did this monarch still have the nerve to stand up to them the way he had done years before as a gutsy teenager with Goliath? Or had he gone soft by now? They sent their raiders into a certain valley in Israel. "So David inquired of God: 'Shall I go and attack the Philistines? Will you deliver them into my hands?'" (1 Chron. 14:10).

God said yes, and David's army moved out, winning a great victory. But later, the Philistines came back to the same valley. "So David inquired of God again" (v. 14). This time God gave a different attack strategy from the first. It involved circling around and waiting for God's signal, "the sound of marching in the tops of the poplar trees" (v. 15). In the end, the Israelites were hugely successful.

Notice that David inquired of God more than once. And again, there was not one statement in all the Law that spoke to this unique situation. David knew he needed specific direction from God about this. He didn't assume that because he had whipped the Philistines once he could beat them any day of the week. Instead, he showed a humble attitude and asked for fresh direction.

Today our Father is always ready, willing, and more than able to guide us through life situations. He rejoices when we inquire of him in a trusting, childlike manner.

The entire pastoral staff at the Brooklyn Tabernacle knows that God has definite, specific plans for our church, and it is vital for us to seek his direction. During each week, for example, I face the need to prepare a message. Does God want me to begin a new series on a certain topic? If so, how long should I stay on it? What specific spiritual truth does he want me to convey to the congregation? Does he want me to give words of comfort this week, or a challenge to greater faith in Christ? What would Jesus focus on if he spoke this coming Sunday? He wants to share his heart with every shepherd entrusted with feeding God's flock.

God tells us, "I will lead the blind by ways they have not known, along unfamiliar paths I will guide them; I will turn the darkness into light before them and make the rough places smooth" (Isa. 42:16). We may not think we are blind— but often we are. We don't see everything. We need God's 360-degree vision. That is what "inquiring of the Lord" is all about.

Sometimes God communicates with us through the "gentle whisper" that Elijah heard on the mountain (see 1 Kings 19:12). These are spiritual promptings, positive or negative, that God gives us. He checks us ever so slightly in our spirit, giving us pause, when we are about to head down a wrong path. Or he fills us with a sense of peace and joy when he approves of the direction we are heading in. It takes spending time with God and a teachable heart to pick up these subtle signals. But we can learn them, for the Scripture tells us that "we have the mind of Christ" (1 Cor. 2:16).

There is also the matter that, in the past, God has spoken to his people through dreams. Four different times God spoke to Joseph, the husband of Mary, in this way (Matt. 1:20; 2:13; 2:19; 2:22). These were specific warnings and directives for the unique situation the parents of the Christ child were facing. God has promised that he will communicate with us, too, in this way (see Acts 2:17, quoting Joel 2:28). Not every dream we have is from God, but we must not rule out the possibility.

At other times God seeks to guide us through little things that happen in everyday life. An old friend calls us unexpectedly. We have a chance encounter with a stranger on the street. An idea pops up in our mind out of nowhere. In each case, something may register as a confirmation or warning from God.

These things most often occur as we live with a humble attitude of "Lord, I'm lacking the wisdom to make these decisions on my own. In fact, I can really mess things up if left to my own devices. I need your insight and direction. As you led the Israelites, lead me. As you guided Rebekah and Joseph and David, guide me. Especially warn me about any situation that may look right on the outside, but in reality is a trap set by Satan."

God will not fail to answer such a prayer. He is all-knowing and all-powerful. He can protect us and steer us. Martin Luther, the great sixteenth-century Reformer, said a spiritually skeptical person, "That you despair of yourself and doubt your own power does not displease me; but this displeases me, that you also despair of the power of God."[1] We must never question God's ability to put us on the right path and keep us there.

Ask, Wait, and Listen

Good decisions are more important than *quick* decisions. Yes, I know our society places value on people who are "decisive." They don't dally around; they go ahead and "pull the trigger" with confidence. Some business guru even said, "Management is the art of making good decisions with insufficient information." As Christians, we need to admit that our knowledge will never be sufficient. God is the only one on whom we can count to see us through these Gibeonite deceptions every time. As we ask, wait, and listen, God will be our faithful guide.

I was reminded of the importance of this truth a few years ago when a major television network wanted to feature our church on a prominent news program. The producer came to see Carol and me and seemed impressed by what was happening, by the troubled lives being changed, and especially by the choir of amateur singers that had won several Grammy awards. He openly admitted he was not a Christian, yet sensed something out of the ordinary. "What's the energy I feel around this building?" he asked.

"That's not energy," I replied. "What you're sensing is God's presence and the love he has put into people's hearts."

As we talked, he said he wanted to focus the story on the diverse nature of the choir, with people representing many nations of the world. This seemed innocent enough, and our music department felt it would provide a great exposure for us to a national viewership at no expense. It would help sell the choir's CDs and DVDs. The producer asked to visit a choir rehearsal so he could see how Carol and the group prepare their music. We told him we would arrange for one of our staff to be his host that evening.

But from the onset I felt a gnawing uneasiness within me. I began to pray about this seemingly great opportunity. The more I prayed, the more convinced I became that we needed to proceed cautiously. I knew the media always have their own agenda, and they rarely put Christianity in a good light. Based on what they might record and how they might edit it, this producer had the power to tell a story very different from the true one.

Some people around me thought I was being overly suspicious. They felt we should jump at this invitation. It would be great for the church.

I wanted some more time. The producer sent an email asking what the holdup was. He repeated his excitement for the story and how sure he was that we would love the outcome.

Only then did I find out from the staff member who had hosted him for the rehearsal visit that he had, during a break, approached one of the singers

> Good decisions are more important than quick decisions.

who just happened to be young, attractive, single, and female. He quickly asked for her phone number. She wisely refused to give it.

Neither Carol nor I have ever regretted saying no to this opportunity for national television exposure. We believe the producer's behavior was a warning from God. It took time, of course, for this kind of thing to bubble to the surface. A quick decision would not have been the right decision.

We must never forget that when Israel spent forty years in the desert, the cloud did not follow them; *they followed the cloud*. Moses trusted totally that God's plan was the only safe course. This did not mean the group was always led to comfortable places with fresh water and palm trees. Sometimes the cloud took them to hard spots. But it was all part of God's plan.

> When we make plans governed merely by our human thinking, we run headlong toward tragedy.

A wise decision requires discernment. One of the gifts of the Holy Spirit we desperately need today is "distinguishing between spirits" (1 Cor. 12:10). This gift, like the others, is for the purpose of building up the church. Some contend that these gifts are not available to us anymore but were limited to a previous era of church history. But no biblical passage warrants such a position. In fact, we need this particular gift more than ever in our time. Satan is out to deceive as many as he can. We need God's X-ray vision to see through his ploys and strategies.

Indeed, the apostle John directly told us to

> test the spirits to see whether they are from God, because many false prophets have gone out into the world.... They are from the world and therefore speak from the viewpoint of the world.... We are from God, and whoever knows God listens to us.... This is how we recognize the Spirit of truth and the spirit of falsehood (1 John 4:1, 5–6).

Something that initially seems like an open door from the Lord can turn out to be a trap. We need to inquire of the Lord and trust the Holy Spirit to help us discern God's plan. Only in this way will we keep from missing out on the good things he has for us.

Notice the seriousness of taking any other approach:

> "Woe to the obstinate children,"
>   declares the LORD,
> "to those who carry out plans that are not mine,
>   forming an alliance, but not by my Spirit,
>   heaping sin upon sin;
> who go down to Egypt
>   *without consulting me;*
> who look for help to Pharaoh's protection,
>   to Egypt's shade for refuge" (Isa. 30:1–2).

When we make plans governed merely by our human thinking, we run headlong toward tragedy. The plans we are sure will lead to great things instead have us ending up back in "Egypt"—a place of bondage we should have been delivered from long ago. We end up back where we started before God ever called us out to his special purpose.

Going beyond the "Sensible"

Granted, God's leading may not "make sense" to us at first. I am sure that more than a few Israelite soldiers questioned the order to march around the city of Jericho once a day and otherwise do nothing. Can't you just imagine their mutterings to one another? "We look silly out here! This is really dumb. And you know the Canaanites are up there on the walls and in the towers studying our every move. They're going to know everything about us. We're losing the surprise factor. This Joshua really is a rookie, isn't he?"

But God had a bigger plan in mind. He wasn't confused at all. He wasn't stalling for time until he could figure out something better. On the seventh day, his victory strategy would be dramatically unfolded for all to see.

I was reminded of this truth back in the spring of 2003 when two wonderful people in our church made an appointment to see me. Mark and Gail McKellar, a forty-something African-American couple, were very earnest in their desire to serve the Lord. Mark worked in public relations for the New York City Department of Parks & Recreation, while Gail served in the finance office at the church.

"Pastor Cymbala," they began nervously, "we don't quite know how to say this, but ... we've been praying about something, and we want to bring it to you. We feel as if God is calling us to some kind of ministry with Native Americans in Arizona."

I sat stunned by their words. It sounded totally out of left field. "Uh, have either of you ever been to Arizona?" I asked, trying to find a trail of some kind here.

"No, Pastor."

"Have either of you ever worked with Native Americans here in the East?" I asked.

"No, Pastor."

This made absolutely no sense to me. I reasoned in my mind that this was a fine and sincere couple who had gone off on a bit of a tangent. At least they had no children to be affected by this upheaval. Still, I as their pastor needed to gently steer them back to reality.

But not so fast! The room was quiet as I felt the Holy Spirit speaking to my heart. *Don't discourage them. I am in this. Just help them.*

I looked up and finally said, "I believe this is from God. Would you like me to make some contacts for you? I'd be glad to see what I can do."

They broke out in big smiles. We prayed together that day that God would lead them in a sure path, even though this was far away both geographically and culturally from all they had known in life to this point.

Mark and Gail made a one-week scouting trip to Phoenix soon afterward. They had only one advance appointment that I had managed to arrange for them. They flew in on a Saturday evening, checked into a motel, looked in the phone book, found a church with the words "All Tribes" in its name, and decided to attend the next morning. They hoped and prayed that God would somehow lead their steps.

The guest speaker that morning was the president of American Indian Bible College in Phoenix. A denominational leader was also there, who took the couple to lunch, listened to a description of their burden, and began opening doors for them throughout the coming week. They visited several reservations and got to meet Indian pastors. They realized that the best avenue for lay workers such as themselves would be to try to become teachers in Native American schools.

Back in New York, they got busy getting their teaching credentials in order. Awhile later they moved to Phoenix. They spent two years as interns at All Tribes Church. Then they both landed teaching positions in the public schools of Holbrook, a town of 5,000 along Interstate 40 just outside the Navajo Nation reservation in northeast Arizona. Gail teaches fourth grade there, while Mark teaches eighth-grade social studies. Many of their students are Navajo.

Every weekend finds them working with the children and youth at a native church in Bidahochi, thirty miles north on the reservation. Friday nights are given to teen outreaches; they drive a van all over to pick up kids whose homes are rocked by alcoholism and drug addiction as well as a huge dose of hopelessness. They have seen many youth come to

Christ in these meetings. On Sundays they lead the children's church ministry. Mark occasionally preaches there as well.

This couple could not be happier. They are exactly where God intended for them to be. I am so glad now that I didn't squelch their vision back in 2003. God's ways were indeed higher than anything I imagined.

If Mark and Gail had been required to take a personality test, I'm sure the results would have been that they "didn't fit the profile." But the early church turned the world upside down without the help of psychological profiles. Had Jesus relied on tests, would he have chosen Peter, the fisherman from Galilee with no rabbinical training that we know of? Yet Peter ended up being the "apostle to the Jews" (Gal. 2:8). He certainly would not have chosen Judas, who became the betrayer. The apostle Paul, with his impressive Jewish education—complete with a diploma from the esteemed rabbi Gamaliel—was chosen by God to be "the apostle to the Gentiles" (Rom. 11:13)! Somebody must have ignored their test scores.

> Had Jesus relied on tests, would he have chosen Peter? He certainly would not have chosen Judas, who became the betrayer.

There is a place for human logic and judgment—but not if these things undermine God's plans for our lives through the ministry of the Holy Spirit. We were made for more. And we will discover that "more" as we ask repeatedly for the Lord to reveal his will. We must never accept that something is good until we have sought God earnestly in prayer. Joshua learned that the hard way at Gibeon. He moved too quickly.

The Bible says that "everything in the world—the cravings of sinful people, the lust of their eyes and their boasting about what they have and do—comes not from the Father but from the world. The world and its desires pass away, but *whoever does the will of God lives forever*" (1 John 2:16–17). Our first priority must always be to learn and then do the will of God. Everything in this world around us will soon disappear. True greatness is found in simple surrender to God's plan for our lives. As Jesus explained the day his family members came to visit him, "Whoever does God's will is my brother and sister and mother" (Mark 3:35). Doing the will of God is how we attain intimacy with Christ.

We can learn the purpose of God as we fill ourselves with his Word and then look to him for direction with a surrendered heart. Soon, doors will open, and we will experience the deep joy of living in the center of God's will.

CHAPTER 7

WHOLEHEARTED FOR THE LONG HAUL

He had attended so many funerals in his time that he had lost count. Everywhere he looked these days, the faces all seemed so young. Virtually no one was left in his age bracket. What did people think when they glanced at his white head or his craggy face? "There's the old guy," he assumed.

We could be talking about Frank Buckles, who at age 107 (at the time of this writing) is the last remaining American who served in Europe during World War I. Fibbing about his age in order to join the Army, he became an ambulance driver in France at age sixteen; his last duty was to escort German POWs back home after the Armistice was signed. He received the French Legion of Honor award in 2004. Buckles still lives on his West Virginia farm.[1]

Or we could be talking about Caleb, that long-time friend of Joshua. Caleb, too, was a gritty old veteran. When people saw his white hair and craggy face, they too may have thought, "There's the old guy." But whenever anyone was willing to listen, Caleb could still retell the dramatic saga of how God pressured the Egyptians with ten plagues to set his people free. He could still see in his mind's eye the Red

Sea rolling up in front of them. He had been a strong young man when the thunder crackled around Mount Sinai and God gave Moses the Ten Commandments. Of course, that was a long time ago....

Caleb had made a name for himself early on by standing firm in the minority. As one of twelve reconnaissance agents sent from the desert to check out the Promised Land, he was the one who interrupted all the naysayers. "Then Caleb silenced the people before Moses and said, 'We should go up and take possession of the land, for we can certainly do it'" (Num. 13:30). Only his friend Joshua agreed with him. They lost the debate that day.

> Caleb was not interested in fudging the lines or seeing where he might cut corners. He had no desire to hesitate or second-guess.

But God never forgot Caleb's bold spirit of faith. He made it clear through Moses on several occasions that Caleb would get "the land he set his feet on, because he followed the LORD wholeheartedly" (Deut. 1:36). That word "wholeheartedly" shows up five different times in relation to Caleb (see also Num. 14:24; 32:12; Josh. 14:8; 14:14). He had a one-track mind (as well as heart and soul) for the Lord. No wavering, no compromise, no negotiating with the purposes of God. There was nothing lukewarm or tentative about him.

Today we need more of that spirit in our culture, which isn't quite sure anymore whether any commitments are supposed to be permanent and unbending. Two people often stand before a member of the clergy and commit themselves to each other in marriage "for as long as we both shall *love*." That way, if they start to feel differently down the road, they have a way out.

To bring children into the world implies the responsibility of providing shelter and food as well as emotional and spiritual nurture to young lives. Yet too often, parents today pull back from their own offspring, caring little for their welfare or actually leaving the household altogether.

Churchgoers profess that they serve Christ and obey Scripture. After all, he did secure pardon for them at a very high price on the cross. But then when they happen not to like something they read or something they hear in a sermon, the waffling begins. They ask whether there isn't an "alternate interpretation" of that particular passage. Surely God didn't intend for that verse to be taken at face value, did he?

Caleb would have had no tolerance for such things. He was not interested in fudging the lines or seeing where he might cut corners. God had promised a great land to Israel, and Caleb's response was, *let's go get it!* He had no desire to hesitate or second-guess. He was wholly committed to the divine plan for Israel.

Unfinished Business

Caleb never forgot the goal—claiming the Promised Land—even as the desert years passed into decades. He was there the day the nation finally entered Canaan, no doubt cheering as loudly as anyone. He saw the walls of Jericho collapse. He helped in subsequent battles. And finally, after some of the dust had settled, he went to see his old friend Joshua about some unfinished business.

"You know what the LORD said to Moses the man of God at Kadesh Barnea about you and me. I was forty years old … And I brought him back a report according to my convictions, but the others who went up with me made the hearts of the people melt in fear. I, however, followed the LORD my God *wholeheartedly*" (Josh. 14:6–8).

There's that word again.

Joshua no doubt nodded in assent. He knew where this conversation was heading. He could tell Caleb was about to raise the subject of a permanent home for himself, after all this waiting. Sure enough ...

"So here I am today, eighty-five years old! I am still as strong today as the day Moses sent me out; I'm just as vigorous to go out to battle now as I was then. Now give me this hill country that the LORD promised me that day. You yourself heard then that the Anakites were there and their cities were large and fortified, but, the LORD helping me, I will drive them out just as he said" (vv. 10–12).

Don't you just love this kind of tenacity! Caleb may have been old, but he had no intention of quitting. He was not afraid of taking on the Anakites (Canaan's most towering, fearsome warriors). He firmly believed his God is stronger, and he would not let loose of the divine promise. His faith was bigger than any fear or scouting report. He meant to possess *everything* God had promised.

Caleb was like the Roman centurion in Jesus' time who asked for his servant to be healed. When Jesus offered to go visit the man, the centurion replied, in essence, "That's not necessary. Just say the word right here, and it will happen. I know it!" He boldly stated the conviction of his heart, so that Jesus "was amazed and said to those following him, 'Truly I tell you, I have not found anyone in Israel with such great faith'" (Matt. 8:10). Yes, it is rare to find people—Jewish,

Roman, American, or any other nationality—who will take God at his word without a hint of reservation. But that is God's desire for us all.

God wants us to say, with Caleb, "My life will be shaped by God's promise and plan, not by my own opinions or rationalizations. What God says, I will believe. Now let's get on with it."

Joshua saw the glint in his old friend's eye. He knew there would be no stopping this warrior. The Bible says, "Then Joshua blessed Caleb son of Jephunneh and gave him Hebron as his inheritance. So Hebron has belonged to Caleb son of Jephunneh the Kenizzite ever since, because he followed the LORD, the God of Israel, wholeheartedly" (Josh. 14:13–14).

Did you know that Hebron was the highest-altitude town in all of Canaan? Sitting at 3,040 feet above sea level, it was higher even than Jerusalem. This was indeed the "hill country" (v. 12), which meant the fighting would be tougher. The hills were infested with gigantic Anakites. Caleb didn't care. He was ready to push against all difficulties to gain the blessing God had for him.

And he was not going to be talked out of it. Nobody dared say, "Don't you think you're maybe a little old for this? How about a nice retirement condo by the Mediterranean instead?" One look at Caleb let people know this man was *still* on a mission.

Sometimes subtle comments and influences from those nearby try to weaken our radical resolve in following Christ. The prophet Micah once spoke about how relatives would rise up against each other on important issues, and "your enemies are the members of your own household" (Mic. 7:6). Jesus quoted this prophecy when he was sending out the twelve disciples for a special ministry tour (see Matt.

10:35–36). He told them to press on boldly despite what others said.

When we began at the Brooklyn Tabernacle years ago, many of our first converts were young Puerto Ricans whose chaotic lives in the neighborhoods were changed by Christ. Every New Year's Eve we held a service to thank God for the blessings of the previous year and to pray for the year just ahead.

You would think that parents would have been happy about these kids finally straightening up. But I remember some of them arriving at that special service almost shaking with fear because their families were so opposed to their presence. Their parents wanted them to be at the family's wild New Year's party instead.

"So what did you do last New Year's Eve?" I asked.

Answers ranged from "I got drunk" to "I got in a fight" to "I was at this party, and they had to call the police."

"Did your family mind that you were out of control?" I asked one young man.

"No—they were part of it!"

> "So what did you do last New Year's Eve?" I asked. Answers ranged from "I got drunk" to "I got in a fight" to "I was at this party, and they had to call the police."

Now that these kids were following God wholeheartedly, their family members were actually upset with them.

It is still hard today for a young person to stand up and serve Jesus. I look at the dozens of teenagers who sing in our youth choir, and I know that most of them will go to school the very next day with metal detectors everywhere. They will have to navigate a gangsta rap culture that promotes violence, resists any kind of authority, and denigrates women. If the teenagers do well academically, they are in violation of what's "hip." They may even get attacked physically for making good grades.

Some of them are mocked for using correct English instead of the slang of the street. When they stand for Christ and live according to God's will, they are quickly marked as odd or weird, according to the majority. How we need to pray for "young Calebs" around the country to hold firm against the flow and press ahead with Jesus.

Willing to Wait

Caleb, of course, had to stay strong-minded for God over a period of four decades. He trudged along with the other Israelites in the desert, until the nation as a whole was in position to be blessed by God. Caleb never gave up, never got despondent, never grew cynical or bitter, and never lost sight of the promise he had received. Instead, he—a man of *great* faith—walked alongside people who had *no* faith. His spirit never grew harsh.

He suffered along with the others for something that was not his fault. Sometimes in life we get penalized along with the majority. We feel like screaming, "Look, I didn't do anything wrong! Why do I have to be bogged down with these people?" It is not fun at all.

But for those who wait faithfully for God's promise to be fulfilled, their day will come. They keep repeating to themselves the prayer of Psalm 130:5–6: "I wait for the LORD, my whole being waits, and in his word I put my hope. I wait for the LORD more than watchmen wait for the morning." Yes, it sometimes feels like being a security guard on the overnight shift, with nothing to do but stare at the clock, thinking the sunrise will never come again. But just wait.... God's timing is sure, and he will not disappoint you in the end.

119

In fact, as Isaiah 30:18 says, "The LORD longs to be gracious to you.... Blessed are all who wait for him!"

Waiting for God can be difficult. Many discouragements and distractions work to pull our eyes away from what the Lord has promised. We have all seen people become bitter and angry because God's clock moved too slowly for them. As a result, they lost out on God's fullest blessing. Caleb showed no signs of irritation during his long, long delay. He stayed full of faith until, at last, his moment arrived.

He also apparently stayed in physical shape. Although an octogenarian, he could say he was still fit to engage in battle. He wasn't about to succumb to the sentiment often heard in our time of "I'm tired now after all these years ... let the younger folks do it ... it's their turn, don't you think?" Caleb had what God described as "a different spirit" (Num. 14:24).

Always Ready for a Challenge

Like Caleb, those who are totally devoted to God never retire. They never get cranky and negative. Instead, they say along with this brave man, "Give me a job to do. Give me an enemy to conquer. I'm ready for a new challenge!" Some of the best ministry, in fact, can be done by those who have finished a normal career in the business world. In many cases God has been preparing them all along for opportunities they never imagined.

Bonite Affriany was fifty-eight years old when she first came to the Brooklyn Tabernacle. A native of Haiti, she was a registered nurse. She heard the gospel, responded to an invitation, accepted Christ as her Savior, and was baptized by me in July 1997. She began to grow in her faith and soon joined our Prayer Band, which intercedes throughout the week for various needs.

Her desire to serve God kept growing. Eventually she quit her job, applied for early Social Security, and began living off that plus her savings so she could give more time to ministry. In 2001 she traveled back to Haiti to buy a piece of land in Jacmel, a town of some 15,000 along the south coast. Its white-sand beaches and art galleries attract some tourists, but most people there live in

> Those who are totally devoted to God never retire. They never get cranky and negative.

abject poverty. Bonite thought she would put up a simple building, organize a feeding ministry for the children, and then return to New York to earn more money that would finance the work.

Every time she prayed about her project, however, Bonite felt a call to go live in Jacmel herself. Once when I was preaching, I began moving toward the section where she happened to be sitting and said I felt God was calling someone in our church to step out on a specific mission. I didn't know who; I was just expressing what I felt God put in my heart at that moment. She listened intently and took this as a confirmation of what she had been sensing in prayer.

This quiet, unassuming woman went out and bought a one-way ticket to Haiti. The first week she started a morning prayer meeting from eight to nine o'clock under a mango tree, putting out coconut leaves to cover the muddy ground so people could gather. The numbers began to grow. Soon she had a simple building completed so the feeding program could begin. Conditions were primitive, of course. The phones often didn't work. Electricity would come and go; on occasion Bonite would endure four or five days with only the light of a kerosene lamp after sunset. But she pressed on.

Two women from our church, Suzan and Janet, decided not long ago to take Thanksgiving week and go see Bonite's ministry for themselves. They returned to New York with amazing stories. For starters, their inbound flight to Port-au-Prince, the capital city, was delayed, causing them to miss the connector flight—the last flight of the day. Bonite's associate, ever resourceful, found a driver with a pickup truck she could hire to take them to Jacmel.

The trip, normally three hours, lasted longer than the daylight, as the truck broke down five times. Of course there were no street lights. The three women and their luggage bounced along in the back of the pickup in pitch darkness. Whenever a vehicle would come up behind them, the staff member would say, "Get down! Don't let them see the suitcases!"

"Why?" the visitors asked.

"Because luggage means tourists. If they see you're tourists, they'll stop the truck and rob us!"

Genuinely concerned by now, Suzan paused to remember it was Tuesday night—prayer meeting night back in Brooklyn. She pulled out her cell phone and called the church. "Pray for us right now!" she pled. "We're in a situation here that I don't want to describe, but ask the Lord to watch over us." This message was quickly passed to me as I led the meeting. I immediately called the congregation to pray on their behalf. Late that evening, the women arrived safely in Jacmel.

By the next morning Suzan and Janet found themselves in the thick of preparing rice and beans plus a small salad for 165 children who depend on Bonite for a meal each day—in many cases, their *only* meal of the day. The women also worked sorting used clothing our church had sent down to Jacmel. They saw a modest learning center in action, where the poor were learning to read and write.

One day the women went to visit a Haitian prison where Bonite often ministers. They told me later, "Pastor, we're not kidding—the stench hit us in the face a good two hundred yards outside the gate. Urine, feces, filth—it was overwhelming! Bonite didn't flinch a bit.

"We went to one cell maybe twelve feet square that had been packed with forty inmates! Some of them hardly had enough clothing to cover up in our presence. We started passing out toiletries and little notebooks—you would have thought we had brought in bars of gold.

"There were two small cots in the cell, but—how in the world did this many men sleep at night? We asked, and they replied, 'We take turns. A few lie down and sleep for an hour while the rest of us stand. Then we trade places.'"

Bonite promptly began preaching the gospel to the men in Creole, her native tongue. They listened respectfully. It was incredibly hot; the two visitors from Brooklyn fanned her to keep her a little cooler while she spoke. In the end, she prayed with the inmates and invited them to welcome Jesus into their hearts.

That evening, back at Bonite's small compound, it was time for church again—a nightly occurrence. The praises of God in Creole rang out into the darkness, followed by the preaching of God's Word.

All this was—and still is—happening because a woman now pushing seventy years of age had chosen to follow God's call wholeheartedly. She hasn't sought the comfortable life. She hasn't dropped out to spend her days watching television or shopping for another pair of shoes. She has elected instead to take the light of God's love to a difficult, needy corner of the world, and she is enjoying the smile of God on her efforts.

Ripple Effect

Bonite's work is bound to bear fruit in the lives of future generations even after she goes to heaven. Who knows what future leaders in the country of Haiti may grow up coming through her food line? When your devotion to the Lord is strong and true—when your faith hangs on, no matter what—the blessing is felt not only in your own circumstance but also in the lives of those to come.

God had promised to Caleb a homestead not only for himself but also for "your children forever" (Josh. 14:9). In fact, the next chapter (Josh. 15) gives some detail about how Caleb transferred some land with a set of springs to his daughter and son-in-law. This water source was part of the overflow of God's blessing upon Caleb.

The more we trust God and follow his assignment for our lives, the more our children and grandchildren will be blessed. Both Carol and I had parents and grandparents who trusted God no matter what. One of my grandmothers, for example, was born in Poland. She met my grandfather in a poor mining town in Pennsylvania and married him there. They came from a strongly traditional religious background, but after they experienced the living Jesus, they began to attend vibrant home meetings. As a result, they were ridiculed in a variety of ways, including garbage being thrown onto their yard. But they remained faithful to God.

They raised a daughter who shared their radical faith—my mother. She held strong even when my father became an alcoholic and lost his job because of it. He was often violent. Relatives advised my mother just to leave him. But she chose, because of her dogged faith in God, to stay and believe for a divine turnaround. That is exactly what happened after twenty-one years of drinking. For the last dozen years of his life, my dad was entirely sober. My mother, now ninety-three years old, has proved that God never disappoints those who wait faithfully for him.

Carol's maternal grandmother lived on a Wisconsin dairy farm with a husband who also drank a great deal and opposed the things of God. Some winter weeknights she would go to church and return home only to find herself locked out in the cold. But she never wavered. And her descendants, including Carol, have been inspired to steadfastness by her example of faith.

Many Christians, of course, do not have such a godly heritage. Some are the first in their families ever to trust Christ. They have the privilege of starting a new ripple effect of blessing that will affect future generations.

When you stop to think about it, you realize that the early Christians in the first century were in uncharted territory when it came to standing strong for Christ. This was a new day altogether in God's plan for the earth. They were rejected by the religious leaders of their time because they preached that the long-awaited Messiah had come. Their activities were considered illegal by some of the governing authorities. They had little money for food to feed them, no technology to help them, no buildings to shelter them, no consultants to advise them, not even a New Testament to inspire and guide them. Yet they forged courageously into the Roman world and "spoke the word of God boldly" (Acts 4:31).

> The more we trust God and follow his assignment for our lives, the more our children and grandchildren will be blessed.

We catch a glimpse of the apostle Paul's all-out commitment in his farewell comments to the Ephesian elders. He tells about his upcoming trip to Jerusalem, how dangerous it is likely to become, and then says, "However, I consider my life worth nothing to me; my only aim is to finish the race and complete the task the Lord Jesus has given me—the task of testifying to the good news of God's grace" (Acts 20:24).

This kind of devotion is so radical, this faith so deep, that it almost takes our breath away. Paul had no assurance that he would come out of his next mission all right. (In fact, he didn't; he was taken into custody there in Jerusalem and spent most of his remaining years in chains.) But it was totally irrelevant to him. He focused instead on fulfilling his calling from Christ.

The authorities, whether religious or civil, really could not defeat Paul, because he didn't care what happened to him personally; it was all about the will of God. He truly was not concerned with living or dying. He wrote to the Philippian church, "What shall I choose? I do not know! I am torn between the two: I desire to depart and be with Christ, which is better by far; but it is more necessary for you that I remain in the body" (Phil. 1:22–24). His devotion to Jesus consumed every part of his being.

The same could be said of others in that century and throughout church history. Wholehearted followers of God do not worry about their comfort level, their retirement, or their reputation among their peers. They seek only to stay on track with their Lord.

Determined, Yet Dependent

As with Paul, we have seen in the life of Caleb that strong determination to serve God no matter what happens. But we can also see a meek side to Caleb. He was more than just a proactive "Type A" personality who liked to fight anyone who got in his way. Notice the all-important phrase in his statement to Joshua about tackling the Anakites with cities "large and fortified, but, the LORD *helping me*, I will drive them out just as he said" (Josh. 14:12).

In other words, this campaign would not be based solely on human bravery. Caleb knew he needed "the LORD helping me" in order to accomplish anything, large or small. The same is true for us. Only with the Lord's help can we conquer the enemies that stand in our way. God's power and grace are required for every challenge before us. We cannot attempt to claim the first half of Philippians 4:13 — "I can do all things"—without understanding the rest of it: "through Christ who strengthens me."[2]

Following God wholeheartedly for the long haul requires us to be totally dependent upon him and his Word. We grasp what he says to us and hold on tightly, refusing to let it slip from our hands and hearts. We then commit ourselves to acting on that promise at every opportunity, whether it comes our way tomorrow or forty years from tomorrow.

Patrick Hamilton, the first Scottish martyr of the Protestant Reformation, was burned at the stake in 1528 in St. Andrews. He was only twenty-five years old. From a wealthy family, he had studied in Paris, encountered the truth of salvation by faith in Christ alone as taught by Martin Luther, and came home to Scotland to spread the gospel. The archbishop chased him away to Luther's Germany, but he soon returned, determined to preach what God had placed in his heart. He was quickly put on trial and executed before his influential friends could rally support for him.

I tell you Patrick Hamilton's story to introduce this marvelous statement of his: "No man can do a greater honor to God than to count him true."[3] He knew that relying on the faithfulness of God mattered more than anything else, and he was willing to pay with his life for that conviction.

Hamilton's murderers expected that his death would stamp out the Reformation in Scotland. In fact, it had the opposite effect. Everyone began talking about what he had stood for. Said one person who had attended his burning, "The reek [smoke] of Mr. Patrick Hamilton has infected as many as it did blow upon."[4]

Wholehearted people like Patrick Hamilton, the apostle Paul, and Caleb make that kind of impact on the world. They unleash the power and truth of God in ways that cannot be dismissed. They take control of territory that others fear to approach. They prove that with God, nothing is impossible.

CHAPTER 8

"WHAT'S UP WITH THIS?"

I was pretty sure I was ready for that first day of basketball practice as a midshipman at the United States Naval Academy. After all, I had been recruited to play there, and I had arrived in Annapolis in fairly good shape. I had even survived the torments of "plebe summer," that six-week Navy version of boot camp that made the new guys (yes, it was all guys in those days) run, swim, march, and do calisthenics for hours on end. In what little free time we had, I played a few pick-up games with some of the better plebe players and knew I could compete at their level.

I had met Head Coach John Mahoney only once, however. We walked into Academy Fieldhouse that October afternoon, suited up, and started shooting around. I felt comfortable with the other guys. This was all familiar territory for me. I wanted to get into a scrimmage of some kind so I, a six-foot guard, could let the coaches see my ball-handling skills and outside jump shot. I looked forward to making a clever pass to a teammate for an easy lay-up, or maybe being able to "shake-and-bake" my opponent.

"Okay, guys, that's it!" Coach Mahoney called out. "Come

on over." And then he added, "Team managers, collect all the balls and get them out of here."

What? We Middies looked at each other in confusion as a dozen or more balls were gathered up and carted out the door. What in the world was going on? How were we supposed to become a basketball team with no basketballs?

"I know you guys want to get out there and show me how you can dribble and pass and score," the coach said. "That's what you came for. But as far as I'm concerned, being in top physical shape is the very foundation of a great season. Here's what we're going to do...."

For the rest of that day's practice we did nothing but defensive drills that didn't require a ball. Down in a crouch, we slid to our left, then right, then left, then right till our thighs burned. We did "suicide drills," where you start on the end line of the court, race to the free-throw line, then back again, then to the center court line, then back again, then to the opposite end, then back again ... over and over and over, until you start thinking suicide wouldn't be such a bad option after all. The coach ran us absolutely ragged. We thought we were already in shape from plebe summer. We quickly found out that he was taking us to a whole different level.

We all limped off the court that day. Heading back into the locker room, I saw a large sign with the now-famous Vince Lombardi quote, "Fatigue makes cowards of us all." I wouldn't admit to being a coward, but I was definitely fatigued that afternoon. By the next morning, I had never known my muscles to hurt so much. Whether Coach Mahoney knew what he was doing was still an open question in my mind.

When You Don't Understand

That certainly wasn't the only time in my life I have been perplexed by a situation that didn't go the way I thought it would—or should. Far beyond the field of athletics, I have faced many a moment over the years that has made me say, to use the current vernacular, "What's up with this? I don't get it."

I suspect you have had these moments in your life as well. In the spiritual realm, God is sometimes harder to figure out than Coach Mahoney. We know God is sovereign and fully in control. We know "the LORD makes firm the steps of those who delight in him" (Ps. 37:23). But what's this latest surprise all about, anyway? When negative things happen to us, when our expectations are left twisting in the wind, when we are crunched by pressures we don't understand, we naturally want to tell God, "This doesn't make sense. I've put my faith in Jesus Christ; I am a child of the King. So why is all this happening? God, what are you doing?"

In his farewell speech to the people of Israel, Joshua brought up just such an occasion. He began by reviewing Israel's national heritage:

> "This is what the LORD, the God of Israel, says: 'Long ago your ancestors, including Terah the father of Abraham and Nahor, lived beyond the Euphrates River and worshiped other gods. But I took your father Abraham from the land beyond the Euphrates and led him throughout Canaan and gave him many descendants. I gave him Isaac, and to Isaac I gave Jacob and Esau. I assigned the hill country of Seir to Esau, *but Jacob and his family went down to Egypt'*" (Josh. 24:2–4).

What is that last half-sentence all about? The rest makes

sense: the call of Abraham to serve God alone and to migrate to this bountiful land of Canaan, the blessing of a son named Isaac, then more generations and growth ... all this is familiar Bible history. But of Isaac's twin sons, Jacob was the chosen one. It was through him, not his brother Esau, that the promised blessing of abundant descendants in a special land would continue. If that promise was true, why did Esau get the hill country of Seir while Jacob and his family got ticketed for Egypt—*away* from the Promised Land?

> When negative things happen to us, we naturally want to tell God, "This doesn't make sense. What are you doing?"

Granted, the high terrain of Seir (southwest Jordan on modern maps) was not as lush as the plains, but it had its advantages. For one thing, it was a lot easier to defend. It was definitely a better deal than having to go down to Egypt, where slavery awaited Jacob's family after some years had passed. So why did his family get the short end of the stick?

The Bible tells us that God's ways are not our ways, nor are his thoughts like ours (see Isa. 55:8–9). As high as the heavens are above the earth, so far are God's thoughts and purposes beyond our comprehension. We have to keep reminding ourselves of this when things don't make sense on the surface.

And sometimes they don't make sense.

A faithful young couple in our church decides to start a family. They are thrilled to find out a child is on the way. Then a month later, the husband gets laid off from his job. Months go by, and he is unable to find work, even though he and his wife pray constantly for employment. What's up with this, God?

In my book *Fresh Faith* I tell the story of Vincent and

Daphne Rodriguez, who adopted a baby girl addicted to crack cocaine. The baby's young birth mother was a working prostitute. This family knew they would have many a sleepless night due to the baby's withdrawal symptoms. But they didn't expect to find later that the baby also had hepatitis C— and learning disabilities.[1] They thought they had done something right and good for this child, the kind of thing God wanted to happen. Why did it turn out to be so hard?

Take courage: The mystifying things that happen in all our lives have several benefits we usually don't see at first.

Unseen Benefit 1:
Hardships Produce Iron in the Soul

The first benefit is that these experiences cause new kinds of growth. The Bible tells us that as times got tougher and tougher for the family of Jacob down in Egypt, "the more they were oppressed, the more they multiplied and spread" (Exod. 1:12). Their population increased to the point that the Pharaoh got worried. He attempted to clamp down on them by ordering the mass murder of all male newborns. It didn't work, of course.

Instead, this adversity produced tenacity and endurance. The Israelites expressed their hope for the future by having more children (one of whom turned out to be the remarkable Moses). They refused to buckle under pressure. Hardship in Egypt produced iron in the soul of this nation.

The idea that hardship produces benefits is difficult for us to appreciate today, surrounded as we are by a culture that shuns any kind of pain, no matter the gain. The goal of most people is ease, comfort, and self-gratification. People find it unreasonable to think that challenges and struggles might be a regular part of God's plan for their lives.

This misunderstanding of God's way is exacerbated by too many television preachers. The airwaves are filled with success formulas (supposedly based on the Bible) that actually pervert God's goal for his people. God predestined us "to be conformed to the image of his Son" (Rom. 8:29), not to be the richest, best-dressed, most comfortable folks on the planet. Solomon and some of the other kings of Israel enjoyed incredible material blessings, yet God sent more than a few prophets to rebuke these men for spiritual and moral bankruptcy. This vital distinction isn't highlighted much in the message of "success"-oriented ministries.

The Bible makes it clear that most believers in the early church experienced nothing that could be described as success. The book of Acts tells how the first Christians were persecuted and chased all over the Mediterranean world. Some of them were killed because of their beliefs. When they faced difficult times, no one stood up and said, "What's wrong with you people? Don't you have enough faith? Just rebuke the devil. Nobody has to die! Stephen's death was unnecessary. He should have just 'confessed' he would live a long, comfortable life. In fact, since God's plan is for everyone to prosper, you all should be living in the biggest houses in Jerusalem. Why are the unbelievers living there? Start claiming those houses and taking them over. Those ungodly people don't deserve them, but we do."

I hope the foolishness of this way of thinking is obvious to you. Paul wrote to one church in a city where he had lasted only three weeks before getting chased out by a mob, "No one [should] be unsettled by these trials. You know quite well that we are destined for them. In fact, when we were with you, we kept telling you that we would be persecuted. And it turned out that way, as you well know" (1 Thess. 3:3–4).

Despite the Bible's clear teaching on this issue, many believers still fall prey to "success" theology. As a result, sincere, Bible-based pastors around the nation are forced to deal with the fallout of this distorted teaching. People come to us confused and frustrated, saying they have followed the formulas but somehow have not gotten the payoffs that were advertised. They sometimes end up questioning their relationship with God and whether the Bible is actually true. "I've been doing what I'm supposed to do," they say, "but God isn't holding up his end of the bargain." Or else they condemn themselves: "There must be something wrong with me. I guess I don't have enough faith."

I want to state clearly that Satan does attack God's people in a variety of areas, including health and finances—and when this happens, we must stand boldly on the Word of God, resisting the devil to make him flee from us. But to conclude that problems and hardship are *automatically* a sign of Satan's harassment in our lives is too simplistic and unbiblical an explanation. We need a knowledge of God's Word and the discernment of the Holy Spirit to know what is really going on. In fact, I am convinced that more often than not, tough times in the lives of faithful believers are indicators that God is preparing them for something special down the road.

> Satan does attack God's people in a variety of areas. But to conclude that problems are automatically a sign of Satan's harassment is too simplistic.

Jesus himself told those who followed him that the life of faith would not be easy. His summary line at the Last Supper, just before heading out the door to Gethsemane and the Cross, was "In this world you *will* have trouble" (John 16:33). He didn't promise his disciples a smooth road. Of course, he went on to declare in that moment, "But take heart! I have overcome the world." When we put the two statements together, we realize that Jesus was saying that God will accomplish his purposes, regardless of the disappointments and bumps that life brings our way.

Trials are part of the Christian territory. God shows us how to avoid some of them, but he walks through others right alongside of us, just as he walked with the Israelites through their time of Egyptian slavery. In many places around the world today, believers understand this exactly—better than we North Americans do. Think of all the brave Christians in Muslim countries who face daily threats of personal harm as well as destruction of their places of worship. The feel-good gospel from North America makes no sense to these faithful Christians, some of whom have to trust God just for enough food to make it through the week.

The mature response to tough times is to affirm, by faith, that God has a purpose in everything he does or allows, even though that purpose might not be clear. Romans 5 has the audacity to ask us to "glory in our sufferings" (seriously!), "because we know that suffering produces perseverance; perseverance, character; and character, hope. And hope does not put us to shame, because God's love has been poured out into our hearts through the Holy Spirit, who has been given to us" (vv. 3–5). It is obvious that God's interest is in spiritual growth more than material possessions.

> Muscles can't build without some force working against them. The same is true in the spiritual realm.

According to several Scripture verses, we should not run from difficult times but rather embrace them, because they make us stronger. We become people of firm character. How do we get that way? By persevering. Persevering through the middle of what? *Suffering.*

That is what I eventually came to believe was Coach Mahoney's philosophy. He wanted to make practices so hard for us Middies that our actual games would seem easy. He had a strategy all along—we just didn't recognize it. We found out later, when we went up against good teams and they ran out of steam about three-fourths of the way through the game. Although they held tough through the first half and into the second, we eventually saw them buckle under our relentless pressure. It was at that point that we could "impose our will on them," to use the coach's phrase, due to their fatigue. They just weren't in condition up to our level.

The principle behind almost any form of exercise is that resistance is required to make a person stronger. Muscles can't build without some force working against them. The same is true in the spiritual realm. Without "powers and principalities" working against us from time to time, our spiritual muscles don't have a chance to be developed.

Jesus told the church at Smyrna, "I know your afflictions and your poverty—yet you are rich!" (Rev. 2:9). Here was a church that had no money, no nice sanctuary, no gymnasium for the youth department, no office suite for the pastors. And Jesus did not say, "What in the world is wrong with you? Where is your faith? Why aren't you claiming your rightful blessings in this world as the 'King's kids'?" Instead, he saw a much different kind of abundance. He defined "rich" in ways that had nothing to do with money. He saw courage and faithfulness under persecution from a "synagogue of Satan" (v. 9) as their true riches. Even more astoundingly, he went on to say, "Be faithful, even to the point of death, and I will give you life as your victor's crown" (v. 10).

That challenge flies in the face of those who attempt to make a long life and material blessings the signs of success-ful Christian living. Even these voices, however, have a hard time making their case in the current environment. Who are the richest people in the world? The list includes plenty of those who have no time at all for God. We really don't want to go down this path, do we? Isn't Christianity about something more important than money, which perishes in a moment?

Never forget that God loves you more than you can imagine. Let that understanding overpower any feeling of confusion or frustration you may have during times of trial. He is building character in you, which is something far more valuable than a big paycheck or a huge house. The ordeals of this life are in fact part of his strategy for producing iron in the soul.

Unseen Benefit 2:
Hardships Drive Us to Prayer

The second benefit to mysterious happenings in our lives is that they give birth to the practice of prayer on a whole new level. When the slavery began and things started getting ugly in Egypt, the Israelites called out to God like never before. This is when serious prayer was birthed among the ordinary people. Exodus 2:23–25 says, "During that long period ... the Israelites groaned in their slavery and cried out, and their cry for help because of their slavery went up to God. God heard their groaning and he remembered his covenant with Abraham, with Isaac and with Jacob. So God looked on the Israelites and was concerned about them."

> At the top of God's priority list is to make us men and women of prayer.

We know that Abraham had been a praying man, and that Isaac and Jacob prayed. But we have no record of their descen-

138

dants calling out to the Lord until they began suffering under the taskmasters' whip in the hot Egyptian sun. This caused them to blurt out, "Oh, God, help us! We need you!"

We do not often think about the fact that it is high on God's priority list is to make us men and women of prayer. He wants us to be people who understand deep inside what praying in faith is all about. He wants people who will pray from their hearts, not just their heads. In fact, this is the only way. As he said through Jeremiah the prophet, "You will seek me and find me when you seek me *with all your heart*" (29:13).

Too much of our praying today tends to be glib and shallow —a mental exercise, a religious tradition. Too little of it evidences a sense of desperation that says, "I must have you answer me, God!" But that is the way the prophet Elijah prayed. That is what Paul meant when he wrote to the Galatians, "I am again in the pains of childbirth until Christ is formed in you" (4:19). That is what E. M. Bounds, the great Methodist apostle of prayer, had in mind when he wrote a hundred years ago:

> Fervor-less prayer has no heart in it; it is an empty thing, an unfit vessel. Heart, soul, and life must find place in all real praying. Heaven must be made to feel the force of this crying unto God....
>
> Prayers must be red-hot. It is the fervent prayer that is effectual and that availeth [*a reference to James 5:16 KJV*]. Coldness of spirit hinders praying; prayer cannot live in a wintry atmosphere. Chilly surroundings freeze out petitioning, and dry up the springs of supplication. It takes fire to make prayers go. Warmth of soul creates an atmosphere favorable to prayer, because it is favorable to fervency. By flame, prayer ascends to heaven. Yet fire

is not fuss, nor heat, nor noise. Heat is intensity—something that glows and burns. Heaven is a mighty poor market for ice.[2]

If Bounds's zeal makes us a little uncomfortable, let us admit how few answers come to our shallow prayers. By contrast, fervent prayer was forged among the Israelites as they suffered. And God heard them and responded. This was one of the good things that developed among the people after "Jacob and his family went down to Egypt."

Compare this fervent mode of prayer with my experience at a recent conference where, ahead of a session in which I would be speaking, I was asked to join the various participants backstage. We formed a circle, and the moderator began praying. I guess he wanted to impress us with his cleverness, so he said, "Well, God, it's great to talk to you again. Let's see, we're going to start this session here in a few minutes, and we just really hope that ..." Pretty soon he was off into a random thought from the Bible: "Lord, it's like I was reading earlier today, let's see, was it Genesis 18 or 19? I'm not sure—it was somewhere around there, you know what I mean...."

My heart was grieved at the flippancy of this mere mental exercise. I doubt anyone in the circle opened their heart to God. This had no resemblance to the prayer the apostle James described as "powerful and effective" (James 5:16).

In contrast, I have heard people pray who could barely articulate words, let alone construct smooth sentences with proper grammar. But their hearts were in tune with God as they cried out in desperation for answers only he could provide. Some of the most powerful prayers are just a one-word cry from the heart: "Help!" Some are not even verbal, but simply a tear that falls from the person's eye.

In Egypt the Israelites learned to pray from their hearts. Rest assured that none of them were saying to God, "Hey, it's great to talk to you again, Lord. I've been thinking today about that thing Abraham said back in Genesis 13, or maybe it was 14...." No, they groaned in anguish, "God, look down at the mess we're in! Have mercy on us! Deliver us, Lord. We have no one else to turn to but you."

Go through the book of Psalms and listen to David pouring out his soul to God. See Elijah crouching with his head between his knees, pleading for rain until the first small cloud appeared on the horizon (1 Kings 18:42–45). Likewise, by the time Israel left Egypt, they knew the power of calling on God. This would do more for their nation than a million-man army.

Andrew Murray, a pastor and prolific author in South Africa in the nineteenth century, once suggested that God's main goal for you and me *each day* is to humble us to the point of drawing us to pray. This sense of weakness is what brings us to the throne of grace, where God can pour out all his wonderful blessings into our lives. Think how much we miss if we live as prayerless people.

With this in mind, we should look at trials and difficulties in our lives as catalysts to bring us nearer to God in prayer. Let Esau and his family have the Seir hill country with all its advantages. Jacob and the chosen people must learn the practice of heartfelt prayer. The Holy Spirit is the one who, according to Romans 8:26, "helps us in our weakness" by teaching us how to really pray in the will of God. When this activity of the Spirit is stifled, God often uses circumstances to reignite it. We don't need to complain about this; instead, let us rejoice and cooperate with the Lord's loving purpose for our lives.

A few years ago in a Dallas church, I preached my sermon

entitled "The Greatest Discovery of All Time," based on Genesis 4:26, which says, "At that time people began to call on the name of the LORD."[3] I included the personal story of our dark two-and-a-half-year ordeal when our oldest daughter was a rebellious teenager, away from the Lord and separated from us. I talked about the Tuesday night prayer meeting where the congregation bore down for Chrissy so intensely that it sounded like a labor room.

At the end of the sermon, I asked people who had wayward children to come forward to pray. Why only study about God's faithfulness without going to the throne of grace for a transaction with the Almighty? I could hear sobbing as people called out to the Lord that day, although this church tended to be unemotional and reserved.

About ten months later, I went back to speak there, this time on a different topic. After the service, a woman came up and greeted me, smiling broadly. "Do you remember what you preached last time you were here?" she asked.

"Yes, I spoke on Genesis 4:26," I replied. "It was about calling on the name of the Lord in the midst of our darkest moments."

Then the woman told me the story of how her own daughter had been straying from God and breaking the hearts of her family. She said my sermon that night had moved her to believe God and boldly intercede for a spiritual turnaround. And God had heard her cries. She joyfully told about the dramatic reversal in her daughter's life.

"Is she here tonight?" I asked.

"Yes! She sits next to me in the choir," she replied, pointing toward the risers, where some of the choir members were still lingering. There I saw a beautiful young lady smiling and waving at me. Her mother and I rejoiced together at the goodness of God.

This painful experience taught this woman to pray at a deeper level. In that, she has gained a priceless treasure. I am reminded of G. V. Wigram, a Plymouth Brethren writer in England, who wrote, "Which would you rather have? A smooth path, or a road so rough that the Lord is compelled to reveal his face to you at every step?"[4] For me, I would rather have the intimacy of knowing Christ in all his love and grace, even if it requires a stony trail to get me there.

Unseen Benefit 3:
Hardships Give Us a Story to Tell

The third benefit when we emerge successfully from a "what in the world is going on?" experience is that it provides a real-life testimony we can share with others. The Israelites who got delivered from Egyptian bondage never stopped talking about it. It became part of their national and spiritual identity.

God told the Israelites to make sure their children caught the importance of the Exodus moment. Deuteronomy 6:20–21 says, "In the future, when your children ask you, 'What is the meaning of the stipulations, decrees and laws the Lord our God has commanded you?'"—in other words, when kids ask the typical kid question about why are there so many rules in life, don't just talk about the rules! Instead—"tell them: 'We were slaves of Pharaoh in Egypt, but the LORD brought us out of Egypt with a mighty hand. Before our eyes the LORD sent signs and wonders.'"

It is so important for the young generation to know that serving God is more than a matter of do's and don'ts. It's an incredible story! It's about the awesome power of God setting us spiritually free when we call upon his name. It's about his faithfulness to us at times when we don't know where to turn. Life's problems are real, but God is more real.

Sharing what we have experienced in Christ can go beyond our local setting. Psalm 105 begins by telling us to "Give praise to the LORD, call on his name; make known *among the nations* what he has done." Later, it gives a detailed recitation of the bondage and miraculous release, sixteen verses in all, ending with "Egypt was glad when they left, because dread of Israel had fallen on them" (v. 38). What an amazing story to tell to people everywhere!

How much more should we share how Christ has proved faithful in our lives. Repeatedly, in the later chapters of the book of Acts, we see Paul telling his personal experience to a variety of listeners — the Jerusalem mob that wanted to stone him (Acts 22), a Roman governor (Acts 24), and King Herod Agrippa and his wife (Acts 26). Paul's story always carried an impact.

We need to realize that what God does in our lives is not just about "me, myself, and I." He is doing things that will overflow into the lives of others through our testimony of his faithfulness. God is always into making his children channels of blessing. Remember this every time you face a difficult challenge. The day is coming when you will be a source of inspiration and hope to someone else who is undergoing a deep trial.

Have you ever thought about who are the strongest Christians you know? To whom would you go if your back was against the wall and you needed someone to go to God with you? Would you approach the person who lives on Easy Street or Problem-Free Boulevard? Or would you go to the person who has been through the fire, the person with iron in their soul, the person who has learned to trust God and hang onto his promises through the worst kind of trial?

How many millions of desperate people down through history have been comforted and encouraged by what God did for the Israelites in Egypt. Take, for example, the thousands and thousands who came to America on slave ships. They had almost nothing to live for in this strange new land of oppression. Yet listen to their songs, the classic Negro spirituals. Notice how often these victims sang about the ancient Hebrews in Egypt. See how their hope was sustained by the expectation that God could do it all again.

> Every time you face a difficult challenge, remember that the day is coming when you will be a source of inspiration and hope to someone else.

This is just one example of how the testimony of Israel's deliverance has echoed through the centuries. But remember, there would have been no liberation story without first the hardship. Without a "what's going on?" experience in your life, there will be nothing going on worth talking about later. God develops testimonies of victory out of settings of difficulty and sometimes even desperation. Then he puts them to use with people who are struggling today just like we did yesterday.

My son-in-law, Brian Pettrey, is on our pastoral staff and was recently working with a thirty-four-year-old man whose business talent was being repeatedly undermined by his addiction to crack cocaine. This man has a college degree in economics and made good money over the years, all of which he smoked away. Although he had grown up in an evangelical church in Georgia and knew much about the Bible, he lacked an understanding of Christ's power to deliver and keep him on the straight path day by day.

Now he was at a point of desperation, out of money and with no place to live. Brian persuaded him to come to a

Tuesday night prayer meeting. There he walked forward and fell on his face at the altar, admitting that his life had come down to nothing. He had made many promises to change in the past, but could fulfill none of them in his own power. He had, as we sometimes say in New York, "turned over more new leaves than the trees in Central Park."

I picked up a microphone that night and said, "Here is a man who desperately wants to get free at last from drugs. How many former addicts do we have here tonight who could come up and lay a hand on his shoulder, asking God to set him free like he did for you?" Dozens of men began to stream down the aisles, each one a testimony to God's amazing power in their personal lives. They began to send up a chorus of what E. M. Bounds would call "fervent" and "red-hot" prayer for this man's deliverance. It was a powerful season of intercession. The victories of the past were put to strategic use here in the present.

The men swarmed him with words of encouragement from their own experience. It actually held up the meeting for a few minutes as they hugged and encouraged him to keep his trust in Christ. I stood back and let this moment run its course while the rest of the congregation sang praises to God for his grace.

The unwanted, troubling, mystifying, "senseless" things that happen in our lives are occasions to instill strength in our character, force us to pray as never before, and give us a testimony to help others in need. Our struggles are simply a sign that we, like the ancient Israelites, were made for more.

CHAPTER 9

THE ENEMY WITHIN

When you turn the page in your Bible from the last chapter of Joshua to the first chapter of Judges, the mood quickly begins to darken. The invincible Israelites, who have been steamrolling every enemy in sight, now start to experience a few hiccups. Although God had charged them to possess the entire land of Canaan, it seems they can't quite get some of the stubborn old residents to move out. "How about if we share the space?" somebody says. "Let's both live here—can't we all just be friends?"

A litany of failures begins in Judges 1:

"The men of Judah ... took possession of the hill country, but they were unable to drive the people from the plains" (v. 19)

"The Benjamites, however, did not drive out the Jebusites, who were living in Jerusalem" (v. 21)

"But Manasseh did not drive out the people of Beth Shan or Taanach or Dor or ..." (v. 27)

"Nor did Ephraim drive out the Canaanites living in

147

Gezer, but the Canaanites continued to live there among them" (v. 29)

The same language appears four more times in this chapter, regarding the tribes of Zebulun, Asher, Naphtali, and Dan. All over the Promised Land, it seems, various Israelite tribes were making *accommodations* with the enemy.

This was definitely not what God had in mind. At the beginning of Judges 2, he sends his angel to rebuke them: "I brought you up out of Egypt and led you into the land that I swore to give your ancestors. I said, 'I will never break my covenant with you, and you shall not make a covenant with the people of this land, but you shall break down their altars.' Yet you have disobeyed me. Why have you done this?" (vv. 1–2).

Nobody had a good explanation.

One of the saddest paragraphs in all of Scripture starts in Judges 2:10: "After that whole generation had been gathered to their ancestors, another generation grew up who knew neither the LORD nor what he had done for Israel. Then the Israelites did evil in the eyes of the LORD and served the Baals," the Canaanite gods.

This shows the human tendency to drift, to cool off, to wander from God and his divine plan. Various denominations have started out with fire and zeal to serve God wholeheartedly ... only to become something the founders wouldn't even recognize within two or three generations. The same can be true in local churches, families, and even individuals over the course of a single lifetime. Everything goes downhill when we accommodate—rather than eradicate—*the enemy within.*

After listing some details about the Israelite slide (vv. 12–14), the text gets to the point of saying that "when-

148

ever Israel went out to fight, the hand of the LORD was against them to defeat them.... They were in great distress" (v. 15). What an odd picture! God was now opposing his own covenant people!

Newspaper editorials of the day would have given geopolitical explanations for what was occurring, but behind the scenes, it was really God's doing. For any Israelite captain to say, "Come on, let's resist the enemy" would have done no good. They needed to get right with God, who was desperately trying to get their attention.

Throughout the book of Judges, the text repeatedly points out God's hand in Israel's defeats:

"... because they did this evil the LORD gave Eglon king of Moab power over Israel" (3:12)

"So the LORD sold them into the hands of Jabin king of Canaan" (4:2)

"The LORD delivered them into the hands of the Philistines for forty years" (13:1; see also 3:8; 6:1; 10:7)

By the end of the book, things have gotten so crazy that the body of a gang rape victim is chopped into twelve pieces and shipped around the country like FedEx packages. (Read the grisly account in chapter 19, if you have the stomach for it.) The book finishes with this death knell: "In those days Israel had no king; everyone did as they saw fit" (21:25). Joshua and Caleb must have been turning over in their graves.

Two Occupants

I see an important spiritual warning here as to what can occur, in miniature, in your life and mine. It takes the form

149

of self-interest and self-gratification, and it is an enemy within.

We know that Jesus saved us to bring us into a new life of freedom and expansion. The Bible calls us "temples of the Holy Spirit" (1 Cor. 6:19). God has sent his very presence to live inside of us, the way his majesty once filled the tabernacle in Old Testament times. He is not just somewhere out there in the heavenly realms; he is "Christ in you, the hope of glory" (Col. 1:27).

That is all rather astounding, I admit, to think that the same God who created the universe now lives inside each Christian. Yet this was God's plan from the beginning. He always intended to display himself in more than just the starry sky, the rushing waterfall, or the soaring mountain range. He meant to dwell in the hearts of his redeemed people.

Too many of us fail to grasp this. We look in the mirror and see ourselves as terribly ordinary. Yet, because of the Holy Spirit's presence inside, we are remarkable people. In the workplace, in the supermarket, or on the street, believers in Christ may look like anyone else, but in fact we are living temples of God Almighty.

This is why we have new spiritual instincts after coming to Christ. We may not even be fully aware of them, and yet we catch ourselves spontaneously praising the Lord or longing for closer fellowship with him. This is all the work of God's Spirit dwelling within us, who "testifies with our spirit that we are God's children" (Rom. 8:16).

The only trouble is ... there is another occupant trying to "share the apartment" with God. The Greek name for this unwanted resident is *sarx*, translated some 150 times in the New Testament as "the flesh." It indicates our lower nature as carnal men and women who have this lingering fondness for sin. The *sarx* is what we are apart from the influence of God's grace. It is the enemy within.

Our sinful nature constantly, even automatically, yearns for self-gratification. It says, "I want everything to be *my* way. I want what I want, right now." The result is what the apostle Paul listed in Galatians 5:19–21, a lengthy inventory of *sarx* behaviors: "sexual immorality, impurity and debauchery; idolatry and witchcraft; hatred, discord, jealousy, fits of rage, selfish ambition, dissensions, factions and envy; drunkenness, orgies, and the like." And this list was written to born-again believers, no less! Yes, several of these behaviors have to do with sex, but certainly not all. They run quite a gamut of wrong actions and motives. "The flesh" shows itself in many different ways, some large and others small. As Savonarola, the fifteenth-century Italian reformer and martyr, said, "Many have been victorious in great temptations, and ruined by little ones."[1]

> God's Spirit dwells within us. The only trouble is . . . there's another occupant trying to "share the apartment."

It would be nice if, at the moment of salvation, God wiped away all traces of these things from our minds and personalities. Unfortunately, it doesn't work that way. We still find it easy to sin, even though we love the Lord. We are locked in a battle with our own negative instincts.

I don't have to think too hard to come up with a personal illustration of this. I will never forget a night on the basketball court during my senior year, after I had transferred from the naval academy to the University of Rhode Island. (Yes, another basketball story—only this time I won't come out so heroic as in the last chapter.) We were in hot competition to win the Yankee Conference and go to the NCAA tournament. We needed to do our best this night against the

University of Connecticut. The game was televised all across New England.

I was our team captain and, as point guard, was matched up against a UConn player I had battled several times before. Suffice it to say we didn't like each other.

I was also known as a Christian. In fact, several ministers had come to see me play that night. They were thinking about doing a cover story on me for their denominational youth magazine. They may have already started toying with a title along the lines of "Christian Player Comes Up Big for Tiny Rhode Island." I had been invited to go out to eat with these men after the game.

The game was tight. The home crowd was on edge, including some fraternity guys in the front row who had had a little too much to drink. Since the Connecticut state line was less than twenty miles from our campus, their fans had shown up strong along with ours.

With about two minutes left, we were up by five points. A rebound was tipped toward the sideline. The opposing guard and I raced to get it, elbowing each other for advantage. At the last second, as we were both crashing out of bounds, I managed to slap the ball off his leg, thus saving possession for our side. We then fell into the crowd.

Then, out of nowhere, without saying a word, he sucker-punched me right in the jaw.

A red light went off inside my head. I turned ballistic in one second. Some of the URI fans tried to grab him. I began clawing my way toward him with mayhem on my mind. Both team benches emptied onto the floor, and the referees had a riot on their hands.

Little fights broke out in the stands as well. I was so enraged I just wanted to hit somebody—*anybody*. I struggled to reach the UConn point guard. I took a wild swing—

and connected instead with the side of a referee's neck. Fortunately, he knew me from previous games. He grabbed me and yelled, "Are you out of your mind?!" The truth is, I was.

State troopers had to come out onto the floor and break up all the fights. My assailant was thrown out of the game. When order was finally restored, I got back into the team huddle, still breathing fire.

"Sit down, Jim," my coach said. "You can't play now."

This upset me even more. *Let me back out there!* I said to myself. I had turned into some kind of wild beast.

I was forced to sit on the bench and watch as my teammates held the lead for the last two minutes without their captain. The win put us in first place in the conference. My adrenaline gradually subsided. I walked into the locker room, still disoriented, and sat for several minutes in my uniform before going to the showers.

A few minutes later, when I came back with a towel draped around me, a team manager approached. "Hey, Jim," he said, "there's some men downstairs waiting to take you out to eat."

Oh, yes — those ministers who had come to see the wonderful Christian point guard.

The shame of everything settled down over me. I was too embarrassed to look them in the eye.

"Go tell them I can't make it," I said to the team manager. "I'm really sorry."

I sneaked out another exit and walked back to my dorm room that night thinking of little else but the tiger inside me. I hadn't even known it was there. Did this mean I wasn't truly a Christian? No, I had committed my life to God, and I knew Jesus Christ had died for my sins. But the "flesh" was still very much alive, too. I had not been promoted into perfect living by any means.

Our "Ugly Baby"

For all of us, this battle is what I call the "other war." It is not the same as what some Christians today call "spiritual warfare," meaning combat waged directly against demonic powers. The battle against the flesh is different. It is important to understand this, given that many believers over the past couple of decades have been quick to blame nearly every problem on evil spirits.

I do not minimize that reality. In fact, Ephesians 6:11 urges us to "put on the full armor of God, so that you can take your stand against the devil's schemes." But the same author (Paul) had in mind something much closer to home when he wrote about the struggle against our own sinful nature: "I have the desire to do what is good, but I cannot carry it out.... What a wretched man I am! Who will rescue me?... I myself in my mind am a slave to God's law, but in my sinful nature [*sarx*] a slave to the law of sin" (Rom. 7:18, 24–25).

Like Paul, the apostle James made the source of our trouble crystal clear when he explained to fellow believers, "Each of you is tempted when you are dragged away *by your own evil desire* and enticed. Then, after desire has conceived, it gives birth to sin; and sin, when it is full-grown, gives birth to death" (James 1:14–15). To put it in other words: We can't totally blame this "ugly baby" in our life on a mysterious delivery from Satan in the middle of the night. It is the offspring of our own "evil desire."

Jesus Christ came to earth not only to pay the penalty for our past sins but also to break the stronghold of the flesh over our lives today. This is God's great salvation. It cracks the grip of sinful, ungodly ways. When the Bible says that "if anyone is in Christ, the new creation has come" (2 Cor. 5:17), it refers not only to the forgiveness of past sins but also to the dynamic of the Holy Spirit helping us overcome the power of the flesh today. As the Scripture declares, "If the Son sets you free, you will be free indeed" (John 8:36). This freedom can indeed be ours!

> We can't totally blame this "ugly baby" in our life on a mysterious delivery from Satan. It is the offspring of our own "evil desire."

Over the years, in waging the "other war" in my own life as well as counseling people in my church, I have learned a couple of tactics that *don't* work. One is to spend time *analyzing the enemy*. The more you think about the flesh, trying to figure out its strategies and processes, the stronger it seems to get. Yes, it is real—but you don't need to strive for a master's degree in "flesh methodology." You are far better off focusing on God's power and presence in your life. This is the road to victory.

A worse waste of time is to seek to *improve the flesh*, to make it try to behave better and not be so rebellious. Some Christians think that if they could just try harder and muster up a little more willpower, they could train the flesh to be less nasty. That's what the Israelites apparently thought. The Baal-worshipers could be "managed."

This approach is useless. You will never change your flesh! It is completely incorrigible. You may coax it into line for a day or two, but by the next weekend it will be "acting out" once again in all its original selfishness. You will be dismayed to hear yourself moaning, "There I go again!" Your most earnest wishes for self-renovation will be dashed.

Nowhere in the New Testament does it say God will

"work with" our flesh. He only speaks about *killing* it (for example, Col. 3:5). The only hope for dealing with the inside enemy is to abandon ourselves to the leadership of the Holy Spirit. That is what Paul meant when he wrote, "So I say, walk by the Spirit, and you will not gratify the desires of the sinful nature [*sarx*]" (Gal. 5:16). This is the point of his bold statements in Romans 8:6 and 13: "The mind controlled by the sinful nature is death, but the mind controlled by the Spirit is life and peace.... If you live according to the sinful nature, you will die; but if *by the Spirit* you put to death the misdeeds of the body, you will live."

> You don't need to strive for a master's degree in "flesh methodology." You are far better off focusing on God's power and presence in your life.

Let me give you an extreme example of the sinful nature's power that happened back in the 1970s, when heroin was the drug of choice around our neighborhood. Back then, if an addict overdosed and died, it actually created a buzz on the street among his friends. "Wow—where can we get some more of *that* stuff? That dope must really be awesome, man!" Of course, they didn't intend to push themselves completely over the edge, but only as close as possible. Talk about the *sarx* leading a person straight to death—apparently the apostle Paul knew what he was talking about.

In this environment, a young junkie checked himself into a Christian drug treatment ministry on Clinton Avenue called Teen Challenge. "I want to get free," he told the intake counselor. "I'm tired of shooting dope. I've had enough of this life." He made it clear that he didn't want to go on the government's methadone program, because that would simply lead to a substitute addiction. He wanted whatever these religious people had to offer in its place.

During the first day and night at the center, the junkie began hearing pieces of the gospel, of course. He heard others say that Jesus Christ could deliver him. *Interesting*, he thought to himself ... but foremost in his mind at this still early stage was *I'm gonna beat this demon! I'm gonna get this monster off my back one way or another. I don't care how hard it is, how sick I feel, how many times I throw up. If I try hard enough, I can do this!*

Twenty-four hours passed, then thirty-six. The young man began to feel truly wretched. His cravings were almost overpowering. His whole body ached for a fresh fix. How would he ever make it through this second night?

"Okay, you guys," he said to the other young men on his third-floor hallway. "I'm going in my room and lock the door. Don't anybody come near me. Leave me alone! I'm kicking this thing 'cold turkey,' and if any of you stick your head in my room, I might break down and beg you to go get me some stuff. So stay away, even if you hear me crying, screaming, or whatever."

As a further measure, the young man talked one of the guys into chaining him to the heavy old-fashioned floor radiator made of iron that brought steam heat into the room. That way, if his will grew weak during the night, he would be physically restrained from running down to Fulton Street and finding a heroin dealer to fix him up. "This will do the trick," he told himself. Now for sure he could not escape.

It was a fall night with outdoor temperatures still in the pleasant range, so no steam was yet being delivered through the plumbing of the old brownstone. Hours passed. The building grew quiet. The young man tried to sleep, but with his hands tied up, he couldn't get into a comfortable position.

He found himself in the battle of his life. He truly wanted

to be free from heroin. He had taken all the precautions he could think of....

When the sun came up the next morning, the young man was nowhere to be found. The Teen Challenge staff began scouring the building. They couldn't find him anywhere. His room was empty; in fact, the door was standing open. And the radiator ... was missing! Entirely gone, jerked out of the floor.

Within a few hours they found the man out in the neighborhood, high on dope—with a radiator in his lap, still chained to his wrists. The call of the drug had been so strong that he simply couldn't keep holding out. The dealers, of course, had been glad to accept his business no matter how weird he looked.

What a tragic picture of the craving of the sinful nature! It says, "Satisfy me! Give me what I want! I won't stop screaming until I get it!" To fulfill this appetite, whether for drugs or for revenge, sex, control of others, or any other addiction, it will go to incredible and shameful lengths, even to the point of full-scale embarrassment.

How many people today are walking through life with an invisible radiator chained to their arm? How many of us have ended up in a ridiculous situation that destroyed all chance of normalcy? That is what the *sarx* does to us.

Twenty years after this bizarre incident, the 1990s arrived, bringing with them a cheaper replacement for heroin: crack cocaine. We were shocked to read one day in the papers about a man on the Lower East Side of Manhattan who stabbed his mother in the back because she wouldn't give him ten dollars for an envelope of crack. She didn't die from the bloody attack, but she was seriously wounded.

On the street, they say about crack, "It has a voice. And when it calls you, you *will* come." The dealers tell their customers, "It's not a question of whether you'll be back. It's only a question of where you'll get the money to come back."

While these examples may seem outlandish, think of all the ways the flesh nature has worked throughout the years to destroy ordinary believers and even prominent ministers of the gospel. This is why the Bible boldly states not even to try to clean up our misdeeds, reprogram them, finesse them, or sweet-talk them into some kind of truce—we must *put them to death by the Spirit*! If this sounds harsh, let me put it another way: The Holy Spirit is a person, our guide, our leader. When we let him control our lives, he arranges for a lot of negative things to fall by the wayside.

> The Bible boldly states not even to try to clean up our misdeeds or reprogram them—we must put them to death by the Spirit!

Thomas Chalmers was a brilliant Scottish preacher in the first half of the 1800s. Perhaps his best-known sermon is entitled "The Expulsive Power of a New Affection."[2] He paints the picture of a somewhat rambunctious young man falling in love with a girl and really wanting to impress her. Some of his rough conduct quickly drops away. He cleans up his manners, his language, and his choice of leisure activities. Why? Because there is a "new affection" in his life.

So it is with us and God. When we truly fall in love with him, we want to please him more than we wan t to keep indulging the old *sarx*. The Holy Spirit draws us in anew direction. We make decisions on a different basis now.

"Help, Holy Spirit!"

Your battle may not be the siren call of illegal drugs. It may instead be "road rage," or Internet pornography, or simple

YOU WERE MADE FOR MORE

laziness when responsibility calls. The truth is, all such things will keep you from experiencing God's best in your life. They are those stubborn enemies on the road to your Promised Land.

When we are in the heat of battle, we need to look up to heaven and say, "Holy Spirit, help me right now! Lead me in the ways of righteousness. I need you this very moment."

Cultivating a victorious life means developing a consciousness of what feeds the spirit versus what feeds the flesh—and then asking God for grace and wisdom. Many of us need to start asking ourselves, "This article I'm about to read—will it enrich me spiritually, or will it simply pamper my flesh and give it what it wants? What about this television show? This movie? Will this strengthen me in a godly manner, or the opposite?"

It is easy to make the excuse that "Well, everybody else does this ... everybody watches that...." But real Christianity has never been about going with the crowd. It has instead been about going against the flow. It is about walking in the light in a world that lies in darkness. Jesus said his disciples needed to be those who would "deny themselves" (Matt. 16:24). They would have the determination, through the power of the Spirit, to tell themselves *no!* If that sounds hard, it is. But what is much harder is to reap the results of hours and days with the flesh in control. Remember that victory comes only from the Spirit's work, not from any external law or regulation.

> Those who would "deny themselves" have the determination, through the Spirit's power, to tell themselves no! If that sounds hard, it is.

Andrew Murray once said, "No tree can grow except on the root from which it sprang."[3] A quality apple tree does not suddenly develop an offshoot branch that produces tangerines. The nature of the root is consistent with the fruit on the other end. Similarly, if we are connected to the divine root, its character will show in our visible lives. But without the Holy Spirit as our source, the flesh will have a heyday. That is why Paul said to the Christians in Galatia, "Are you so foolish? After beginning with the Spirit, are you now trying to finish by human effort?" (3:3).

The flesh is ever lurking. But as the Spirit was the one who gave us our new birth in Christ, likewise he will keep us safe.

Every day—and throughout the day—we have a choice. Will we accommodate the flesh, or will we draw near to God in full dependence on his power to keep us? If we take this second option, we will find that our words and actions will be different. We will crave times of meditating on the Word of God, seeking a closer relationship with him. We will sense urgings to serve others and help them in their spiritual battles. These will not feel like obligations but instead like opportunities. The source of these positive, holy cravings is not us. Rather, it is a case of "God who works in you to will and to act in order to fulfill his good purpose" (Phil. 2:13).

The way out of anger is to be led by God's love. The way out of sexual temptation is to have the Holy Spirit's purity repel it. When we live by the Spirit, he comes to our aid by deadening the flesh. Meanwhile, we are acutely conscious of the Lord's presence. Our hearts and minds are open for his promptings to do what is right. And we receive the strength we need to deny the flesh and its unholy desires.

The Word of God makes it clear: "Sin *shall no longer be your master*, because you are not under the law, but under grace" (Rom. 6:14). The Law of God tells us what is sinful, but it is powerless to give us victory. That is why the

Israelites drifted away from God and struggled against his representative, Moses, throughout their journey in the desert. And that is why Christ came with his ministry of grace that lifts us up beyond the cravings of our lower nature. He who promised us mastery over the flesh will also fulfill it through his indwelling Spirit.

That is the only way to win the "other war" and defeat the enemy within.

CHAPTER 10

OBJECTION
OVERRULED

If you have ever sat through a courtroom trial or even watched one on a television drama, you are familiar with how defense attorneys react when they don't like something the prosecutor is doing. "Objection, Your Honor!" they interrupt. "Counsel is leading the witness...."

The judge listens to the complaint and decides whether or not it is valid. If the judge agrees, the line of questioning is stopped. But if the judge disagrees, the reply will come down from the bench, "Objection overruled." It is the magistrate's way of saying that the protest was unwarranted, and the trial should proceed.

Sometimes in my Christian walk, when I sense God is trying to do something new in my life, I find myself responding like a trial attorney. Maybe you do, too. We say to God, "I object." We don't do this just to be difficult or defiant. We think we have a valid reason not to step out in faith and obedience to what God seems to be saying. Our reservations are very logical, at least in our minds. But because God loves us and wants the best to come to pass in our lives, he responds with the simple phrase "Objection overruled."

YOU WERE MADE FOR MORE

That was certainly the case with Gideon. He was an obscure farmer whom God tapped for leadership when the nation of Israel, once again, fell away from serving the Lord and ended up in horrible bondage to the Midianites. Every year when the Israelite crops were ready for harvest, the Midianites swept down and stole them. Then one day the angel of the Lord appeared to Gideon as he was "threshing wheat in a winepress" (Judg. 6:11) for fear that the Midianite raiders would find him.

It's hard to imagine today what a desperate act this was. Threshing in those times meant beating the harvested wheat stalks with a rod or flail to knock the kernels loose from the surrounding husks, then tossing everything into the air with a pitchfork. The wind blew the lightweight husks and stalks away, while the heavier grain fell back to the ground for collecting.

And Gideon was trying to do this job down in a winepress —a small pit in the ground where grapes were trampled to extract the juice. Talk about cramped quarters! A modern equivalent might be trying to sand and refinish a large piece of furniture in a bathroom. Your elbows would be bumping into walls and cabinets every five seconds. You would be totally frustrated. You would be shouting, "I need more space!"

So it was for Gideon when the angel showed up with his strangely optimistic greeting, "The LORD is with you, mighty warrior" (v. 12).

Who, me? Gideon no doubt thought. *Do I look much like a mighty warrior?* He promptly voiced his irritation and the first of four objections to the messenger from God.

Objection 1:
"Where Have You Been?"

You can almost hear the sarcasm in his tone when Gideon says, "Pardon me, my lord, . . . but if the LORD is with us, why has all this happened to us? Where are all his wonders that our ancestors told us about when they said, 'Did not the LORD bring us up out of Egypt?' But now the LORD has abandoned us and given us into the hand of Midian" (v. 13).

I encounter people on a regular basis who, like Gideon, are just a little upset with God. He hasn't come through for them, they say. He seems to help other people in other places, but not them. Others get their prayers answered, but for some reason theirs go ignored. They try to tell me that God isn't paying attention, or he is showing up too late to do any good.

The problem for these people is often a case of short-sightedness and limited perspective. People are too quick to blame God for being unavailable. They are like Gideon saying, "The Lord has abandoned us," when in fact it is the other way around. The people of Israel had abandoned God to worship the Canaanite idols. Now they reaped God's chastening for their spiritual infidelity.

> People are too quick to blame God for being unavailable. They say, "The Lord has abandoned us," when in fact it was the other way around.

It is curious to me that in this moment, the angel of the Lord *did not try to defend God*. He didn't even dignify Gideon's taunt with a response. The next words out of his mouth instead are, "Go in the strength you have and save Israel out of Midian's hand. Am I not sending you?" (vs. 14).

Some questions and complaints don't need an answer. Any good parent knows that, and certainly our heavenly

Father does. God's response to Gideon's first objection is get back to the main subject of what he wants Gideon to do *now*. Never mind rehashing the past. There is a job to be done, and Gideon is the divine choice to tackle it.

Objection 2:
"I Don't Have the Right Connections"

Gideon begins to recite how unqualified he is. "Pardon me, my lord, ... but how can I save Israel? My clan is the weakest in Manasseh, and I am the least in my family" (v. 15). He is sure that God needs someone with better qualifications and connections than him. His résumé doesn't look that impressive. His list of references seems woefully short. The Israelite joint chiefs of staff are not exactly searching for a guy like Gideon to lead the charge against the enemy.

What Gideon focuses on is not God's omnipotent power but the insignificance of his life and family. I can empathize with this very deeply. When I first sensed God's call to the ministry, I struggled for many months. I could not envision myself preaching. I had never taken a homiletics course, nor was I a public speaker. I objected as Gideon did, saying to God, "You must have the wrong person."

God's response to me was the same as his response to Gideon that day long ago: *"I will be with you, and you will strike down all the Midianites together"* (v. 16). He was saying in essence, "You may not have the right connections—*but you have me!* I'm your source. I'm the one you need to call. I'll be with you every step of the way." The key to victory is not who we know on a first-name basis, how many phone numbers or email addresses we've collected, what associations we're members of, or which credentials hang on our wall. We belong to God, and we can be confident that he knows perfectly what the future holds. He is not depending on our credentials but rather calling us to rely on him.

George Whitefield (pronounced "*Whit*-field") was born into a poor family in Gloucester, England, in 1714, the last of seven children. His father died when he was only two years old. The boy contracted measles at age ten, which left him noticeably cross-eyed. He dropped out of school for a while to help his mother run the family inn. The only way he got into the expensive and prestigious Oxford University was as a "servitor," meaning he earned tuition money by polishing shoes and carrying the books of wealthier students. It was there, however, that he met the Wesley brothers, John and Charles, and joined their "Holy Club."

Whitefield went on to become the most powerful preacher of the eighteenth century. He made seven different tours of the American colonies and was a major catalyst of the awesome spiritual revival called the First Great Awakening. His name, say some historians, was the most famous up and down the colonies until another George (Washington) came to prominence. Detractors criticized him and made fun of his crossed eyes, calling him "Dr. Squintum." But Whitefield didn't care; he just kept preaching—some 18,000 sermons in his lifetime, many of which were delivered in the open air. When he preached in Philadelphia, the esteemed Benjamin Franklin surveyed the crowd and calculated it to be around 20,000 people, all within reach of his powerful, unamplified voice.

> God says in essence, "You may not have the right connections—but you have me! I'm your source. I'm the one you need to call."

In fact, Whitefield stayed on American soil until his death in 1770. He is buried under the pulpit of Old South Church (Presbyterian) in Newburyport, Massachusetts, just up the coast from Boston. Neither humble roots nor physical limitations kept him from accomplishing what God called him to do. His continual reliance on the Lord is shown in this statement: "God is not only a help, but a *present* help; the gates of the New Jerusalem stand open day and night."[1]

Many of us today are in danger of missing out on a great future with God because of our concern over qualifications. We instinctively say, "I can't," whenever God wants to thrust us out into a new sphere of ministry and blessing to others. We worry about not being able to answer every question that arises. Or God directs us to a larger involvement in our own church, and we say, "What if I do it poorly, and fail? I would be so embarrassed."

Some people will do anything to avoid taking a risk. They will say they are too young, or too old. They will claim they haven't received proper training, or they have a physical limitation. If they are women, they may say God should be calling a man for this job instead. But God knows what he is doing, and when we take the risk to follow him, he will meet all our needs. If we need financial resources, he will supply them. If we need strength and endurance, he will fortify us. If we need wisdom, he has promised to give it to us. We simply have to take God at his word, trusting and obeying, regardless of the what-ifs and regardless of our fears.

It has been wisely said that no place in this world is safer than being at the center of God's will. Conversely, nothing is worse in life than huddling in a "safe" place that God never ordained for us.

Gideon did not step forward immediately to challenge the Midianites, but he did take the first tentative step by going to get a sacrifice—goat meat and unleavened bread—to present as an offering. The angel touched it with the tip of his staff, setting it ablaze. That night the Lord gave Gideon a small assignment to get started. He wasn't asked to knock down all the idolatrous altars in the country—just the one in his father's courtyard. Gideon was afraid of being seen, so he did the job in the dead of night.

Soon he was ready to start assembling an army. However, he still wasn't confident about where God was taking him.

Objection 3:
"Would You Give Me a Sign?"

Gideon decided to put God to a clear-cut test. I don't recommend this practice for anyone. We ought to be able to take God at his word alone, without asking him to prove anything. Yet Gideon laid out a wool fleece and asked that by the next morning it be wet with dew while all the surrounding ground would be dry. How odd that the mere mortal was checking up on whether the all-powerful God was up to a challenge!

Believe it or not, God was gracious enough to accommodate Gideon's request. He didn't need to, of course, but he went along with Gideon's little game. "Gideon rose early the next day; he squeezed the fleece and wrung out the dew—a bowlful of water" (Judg. 6:38). If there was any lingering doubt that God was alert and paying attention to Gideon, this should have laid it to rest.

Objection 4:
"How About *Another* Sign?"

Can you believe that Gideon had the nerve to run his little test *again*? This time he asked for the reverse: a dry fleece and wet ground. I am surprised God did not lose patience with him, saying, "Gideon, you're stalling. You know exactly what I have called you to do, and you know I am up to the challenge of making you successful. Now *get moving!*"

But God did not. He once again gave Gideon the sign he requested. God's mercy and goodness to this man apparently knew no limits. He was not about to give up and find somebody else.

A Swiss theologian and church historian named J. H. Merle d'Aubigné wrote in the 1800s, "God, who prepares his work through the ages, accomplishes it by the weakest instruments, when his time is come, that the work may be seen to be of God and not of man. To effect great results by imperceptible means, such is the law of God."[2]

This has been God's merciful pattern through the centuries as he has dealt with faulty vessels of clay.

The Reluctant Choir Director

I need look no further than my wife, Carol, to find a modern example of God using a hesitant person. She was never trained to read music, let alone write it. She has always found it extremely difficult to stand up in front of a crowd. I remember during our first pastorate in Newark, New Jersey, when she hesitantly invited a few women to come over to our house to form a singing group. Carol was so nervous about the rehearsal that she couldn't eat the entire day. She actually threw up before they arrived—and again after they left!

Carol has said to me privately more than once, "Why is it that God called me to a ministry that often involves things I find so hard to do?" I have had to talk her out of resigning from the Brooklyn Tabernacle Choir dozens of times. She agonizes over things that many others wouldn't think twice about.

One time I happened to go with Carol to a retreat in Nashville sponsored by her recording company. It was a low-key affair for artists simply to pray together and get to know each other. At one point a group of a dozen or so sat in a circle. The moderator asked for each one in turn to say a few words about what he or she did and why.

Carol looked at me across the circle as if to say, *Jim, if you love me ... get me out of this! I can't do this*. They were not asking for a lecture on Einstein's theory of relativity. All they expected was an informal sharing from the heart. Well, it so happened that before Carol's turn came to speak, there was a lunch break. She didn't go to eat. I went up to the hotel room and found her shaking and in tears. "I can't do this," she cried.

> Carol has said to me privately more than once, "Why is it that God called me to a ministry that often involves things I find so hard to do?"

I also remember the first time we rented Radio City Music Hall in Manhattan for a concert and gospel outreach. The hour came when those massive stage elevators would lift Carol and the choir up three floors to appear in front of 6,000 people, where she would have to turn and give a brief welcome before the first song. She froze—and almost fainted.

Yet God has called Carol to a ministry that requires her to stretch. Just like Gideon, she has raised vigorous objections. Her objections have consistently been overruled. Today she leads a choir of nearly 300 voices. In 2005, this woman who always wanted to avoid the spotlight walked out onto a Los Angeles stage to collect her sixth Grammy Award. Every year she leads a music conference attended by about a thousand other musicians, most of whom have far more training than she does.

Carol has grown more confident in God. In church services it is not unusual now for her to take the microphone, totally unprompted, to give the people an exhortation she feels the Lord has given her. She would never have done that earlier in our ministry. She is more willing than ever for God to push her outside her comfort zone. Every time she does this kind of thing, it is an act of faith on her part. She has to look away from her weakness and reluctance, focusing instead on the God of all strength and confidence.

If God's Spirit is upon you, no résumé is too weak. If God is calling you to something more, your perceived lack of qualifications is no longer relevant. God's strength is far greater than your weakness. God's grace is much stronger than your fears. And his plan is not subject to your objections.

Faith for the Battle

After working through his objections with God, Gideon went out and won a spectacular victory over the Midianites in the most unusual manner. God trimmed his force from 32,000 volunteers down to just 300. They went into battle only with trumpets and with jars concealing torches inside. It was another ridiculous war strategy like the one Joshua used back at Jericho. Yet, when they broke their jars to reveal their lighting in the middle of the night and began blowing their trumpets as if it were New Year's Eve, the Midianites thought for all the world that they were surrounded by a massive army. Pandemonium broke loose. In the flickering shadows, the Midianites jumped up and began hacking *at each other* with their swords. They ran for any escape they could find, dashing toward the Jordan River.

Gideon sent word to the nearby Israelite towns and villages for reinforcements to help close off the various roads.

By the end of the engagement, "a hundred and twenty thousand swordsmen had fallen" (Judg. 8:10). The onetime-hesitant farmer had turned into a brilliant general, setting the land free of its oppressors.

Gideon even wound up with his name enrolled in the Faith Hall of Fame along with national heroes such as Enoch, Noah, Abraham, and Moses. Hebrews 11:32–34 says,

> And what more shall I say? I do not have time to tell about Gideon ... who *through faith* conquered kingdoms, administered justice, and gained what was promised ... *whose weakness was turned to strength;* and who became powerful in battle and routed foreign armies.

We don't normally think of Gideon as a great man of *faith*. That word itself appears nowhere in the Judges 6–8 account of his life. We more naturally associate the word "doubt" with Gideon. Yet the New Testament affirms that what he accomplished was done *through faith*. That is what turned his weakness into strength. He eventually believed that God could be trusted, and he stepped out in faith to do what God had asked.

I find it interesting that we Christians are often confused about what to do when our faith is weak. We clearly understand that God is our source for other things. For example, when we struggle to obey his command to love our neighbor or turn the other cheek, we pray, "Oh, God, give me more love. Pour your love into my heart so I can overcome this resentment."

Likewise, his instructions for us to be humble, to share with others, to forgive—these are all hard for us at times. What do we do? We run to God and say, "I'm willing to do this, but I need your grace. Please make me able to follow through."

When it comes to faith, however, we think for some reason that we have to solve the shortage all by ourselves. We have to "try harder." We have to muster up faith from within ourselves. We have to psyche ourselves into a heightened state of believing.

That is *not* how the desperate father of the boy with convulsions thought when he came to Jesus at the foot of the Mount of Transfiguration. The father openly stated, "I do believe; help me overcome my unbelief!" (Mark 9:24). He admitted that there was a piece of unbelief in his mind that he could not whip, and he pleaded with Jesus to help him. Such honesty did not disqualify him at all; in fact, it resulted in deliverance for his tormented son.

> When it comes to faith, we think for some reason that we have to solve the shortage all by ourselves. We have to "try harder."

The disciples made only two major requests of Jesus during their long time with him: "Lord, teach us to pray" (Luke 11:1) and "Increase our faith!" (Luke 17:5). This second request led immediately to Jesus' analogy of the tiny mustard seed. Faith is like that, he said; it may start small, but it can uproot strong trees before it's finished.

If your faith is weak and you feel overwhelmed by what God is proposing for you to do, spend time in the Bible and at the throne of grace, saying, "Lord, I know I should believe you; I know you keep your promises in your Word. But I'm feeling overwhelmed by what I see. It's too big for me. I can't imagine it happening. Help me, Lord! Give me faith to believe."

The Bible clearly includes a special kind of faith in a list of the Spirit's gifts (see 1 Cor. 12:9). That alone ought to tell us that we don't have to manufacture any kind of faith by ourselves. God is waiting and wanting to impart it into our lives. We don't need to struggle. Moreover, we don't need to chant the name-it-and-claim-it mantra of "I believe! I confess this pain in my body does not exist! I am an overcomer!" Get the focus off of "I" and turn your attention to the source of all goodness and power. Run to God and his Word for the faith you need.

More than once during the high-pressure days of relocation to our new church campus, when I felt overwhelmed by the urgent financial requirements, I simply retreated to an upstairs room of my house to sit with my Bible in God's presence. "Lord, I feel beat up," I would pray. "There's no end to the cost of this project; every week is a new demand. God, just feed my soul today. Give me fresh faith for this day." I would open the Word and read it for hours, asking God to make it alive in my spirit. The truths of Scripture and the dramatic stories of God's deliverance would overcome my trepidation. I could stand up and drive to the office with renewed confidence in a God who promised not to fail.

How Faith Actually Works

Faith is more than just mental affirmation. It is more than a theory. It is a deeply spiritual, even supernatural, conviction down in your soul that God can be trusted to do what he said he would do.

Three things happen in the development and operation of faith:

1. God's Promise Possesses Us

When we are possessed by God's promise, we can overcome negative feelings and what our sense of sight often tells us. Like Joshua and Caleb back at Kadesh in the desert, the promise of God towers over the obstacles scattered across the landscape. The promise of God proves stronger than our fluctuating emotions. We are locked in to his guarantee; it controls us.

It is not just a case of seeing a little improvement and saying, "Oh, now I really believe!" Some people pray for their wayward children, and if they sense a bit of softening or openness, they get excited ... but if there's a turn for the worse, they fall into despair. By contrast, those who are anchored in God's promise keep their eyes on God and are *sure* he will come through. They know that "the one who calls you is faithful, and he will do it" (1 Thess. 5:24).

2. God's Plan *Possesses Us*

Being possessed by God's plan helps us rise above our limited human wisdom. Gideon got to the point of accepting that God's battle strategy could be trusted. Only 300 men? Well, okay—if that was what God said to do, Gideon would go along. This was one of the key moments in the *faith walk* of this man.

Our intellect fights against this kind of thing. We often think we have a smarter idea. But God's plans frequently involve risk, whereas we are "risk-averse." If he doesn't work within the time frame we want, we can fall back into the error of planning things ourselves. This kind of behavior is clearly not a work of faith. Only a radical, desperate faith will hold us in times of uncertainty.

3. God's Power *Possesses Us,* *Rather Than Our Own*

God's power transcends our self-effort as well as our desire for "a piece of the action." God ends up getting all the credit this way. The result is something only he can accomplish.

God is the same yesterday, today, and forever. He loves us more than we can imagine. And he calls all of us to play a role in building up his kingdom on earth. He still overrules our many objections and bids us to trust in him alone.

To hold back from following the Lord's sometimes bold initiatives may seem like the safer route—but we will never be happy or find fulfillment that way. The deepest experience of joy in life comes from being in the center of God's will, no matter how precarious that may seem.

Whenever God directs us in a new way, even if it seems scary at first, we need to surrender to his purposes. He will be right there with us everywhere he leads. We were made for more. We cannot let our fears and hesitations keep us from accepting God's wonderful call, which is always greater than we can imagine on our own. Not in our wildest fantasies could we devise a way to chase out the Midianites that oppress us. But God can. He simply asks for our cooperation.

MORE THAN
YOU'D EVER DREAM

The farther you read in the book of Judges, the worse it gets. Gideon's son murders all of his brothers in a deadly power grab. Jephthah makes a thoughtless vow that costs his precious daughter's life. Samson, empowered by God to do great things, keeps fooling around with Philistine girl-friends. A feud between the tribes ends up causing more than 40,000 deaths. As I said earlier, this is probably the most depressing book in the Bible.

Yet one of the world's most heartwarming stories—the book of Ruth—comes out of this very same era. It begins, in fact, with these words: "In the days when the judges ruled...." It is as if the camera zooms in past all the craziness and bloodshed to focus tightly on one simple family. A man named Elimelek takes his wife, Naomi, and their two young sons to the neighboring country of Moab to escape a famine. Elimelek dies early, but the boys grow up and marry local girls. Tragically, both sons come to early deaths, too—we don't know how. Overcome with bereavement, Naomi decides to go back home to Bethlehem in Israel.

Here is where the story starts to brighten up. Both

daughters-in-law love Naomi enough to want to pull up stakes, leave their home in Moab, and go with her. One, named Orpah, lets herself be talked into staying home with her relatives in Moab. But the other daughter-in-law, Ruth, clings tightly to Naomi, determined to follow her to a strange land and keep her company.

The first weeks and months are tough for the two women; Ruth has to scavenge for food to keep them alive. They go on honoring the Lord regardless. Ruth does her tedious work—gleaning leftovers in the grain fields—without complaining. Eventually, a wealthy Prince Charming named Boaz notices her. Love blossoms, and she becomes his wife. They have a little son—Naomi finally becomes a doting grandmother!—and the son grows up to have a grandson, who grows up to have a great-grandson who turns out to be Israel's greatest king.

All of this took place "in the days when the judges ruled," no less.

God Always Keeps a Remnant

I love the fact that no matter how ungodly the world becomes, some people still maintain their devotion to God and one another. No matter how much betrayal and debauchery we see on every side, some people still believe in duty, love, and honor. God is faithful to bless those whose hearts are attuned to him. They may not be in the majority; in fact, they usually are not. But they don't mind; they keep on doing the right thing.

Many times today, those who love the Lord with all their heart and are sincere about following him feel bereft and alone. They look around at the corruption both outside and, unfortunately, inside the church, and they say, "How can people act that way? Don't they know any better?" The enemy often tries to get us to give up and compromise ourselves.

In such a moment, we need to hear God's voice reminding us of what he told Elijah at a low point of discouragement: there were still 7,000 others who had not bowed the knee to the idol of Baal. Elijah was not the only one after all.

Jesus said, "Wide is the gate and broad is the road that leads to destruction, and many enter through it. But small is the gate and narrow the road that leads to life, and only a few find it" (Matt. 7:13-14). God is looking for people in every age who choose his small gate and narrow road. They want to please him regardless of how opposite the cultural tide is running. They will be his holy remnant.

On these God will pour out his abundance in surprising measure.

Just Ordinary People

Naomi and her family were nothing special in the Israelite society. The Bible says nothing about them being descended from any famous personalities. They held no public office. They didn't appear to own a successful business. When Naomi and Ruth arrived back in Bethlehem, nobody took them under wing or set them up in a comfortable lifestyle. In other words, they didn't have social connections to leverage anything.

Yet the Holy Spirit decided to put their story in the Bible. Otherwise, we would never have known about them. I dare say no archaeologist will ever discover an ancient monument in the Holy Land with their names etched on the side. But greatness and renown in God's eyes is a different matter.

What the world calls great is often an abomination to

God. And what the world laughs at—devotion, consecration, faith—is what God calls great. Greatness should not be measured by whether you get your name in *The New York Times*. What heaven is registering has little to do with what happens in the stock market, on the Broadway stage, or at the next Olympic Games. Heaven is more interested in those who live for God every single day, doing the right thing in ordinary circumstances. Those who show gentleness, kindness, and trust. People like Naomi. People like Ruth.

The everyday decisions of life—how we act on the job, how we pay our bills on time, how we give to God's work, how we treat our children, how we care for our relatives, how we respond to adversity—these are the things God is watching.

> Greatness should not be measured by whether you get your name in *The New York Times*.

The longer we walk with God, the more we realize that greatness lies in the small aspects of life. It is perfectly all right for us to be ordinary and unacclaimed in this world. God knows what is truly going on, and he values the common person of integrity.

I stood recently at the graveside of a man named Carlo Boekstaaf. For a quarter century he was a faithful associate pastor at our church. Born in Suriname on the coast of South America during the colonial period, he got his basic schooling in the Netherlands and then immigrated to America as a young man. He worked in his family's printing business at first. One night while watching a Christian television program, he gave his heart to Christ.

Carlo began serving in our church's prayer ministry, led home Bible studies, and in time headed up our lay training department. Eventually it became clear that God wanted him in full-time work as a pastor.

Carlo never got to attend seminary, he never wrote a book, and he wasn't featured as a speaker at big conventions. Yet he was possibly the kindest, godliest man I've ever known. He was a man of prayer and integrity, and he had a caring spirit to take time with people. In his own unassuming way, he greatly influenced our congregation. We feel his absence deeply.

Ordinary people can make an extraordinary mark as they yield themselves to the purposes of God. They don't need to try to pump themselves up. They simply live and serve with honor and diligence, letting God accomplish what he called them to be, whether small or great.

God Comes Through
for Those Who Trust Him

While it takes some time in the book of Ruth before things start to break positively (almost halfway through the chapters), God was not about to neglect these people. He blesses their faith and trust. Ruth and Naomi are examples of "those who through faith and patience inherit what has been promised" (Heb. 6:12). Although they trusted God, they didn't get a payoff in the first five minutes. They had to endure the hard times with patience.

Take Naomi, for example. To lose your husband *and* your two sons prematurely is almost more than any woman should have to bear. She ended up far away from home in Moab without a blood relative in sight. But God gave her a daughter-in-law who was simply wonderful. By the end of the story, Naomi has a stable life on home turf again. And she has a grandson who is the talk of the town.

The women said to Naomi: "Praise be to the LORD,

who this day has not left you without a family guardian. May he become famous throughout Israel! He will renew your life and sustain you in your old age. For your daughter-in-law, who loves you and who is better to you than seven sons, has given him birth." Then Naomi took the child in her arms and cared for him. The women living there said, "Naomi has a son!" (Ruth 4:14–16).

Can't you just imagine the big smile on Naomi's face? God rewarded her faithfulness and confidence in him.

Or look at Boaz, the man who married Ruth. He had built a prosperous farm, with multiple employees. His business interests were doing fine. He was well regarded in the town gate, which was the commercial hub of that economy. He was an honorable man who treated people with kindness. Still, he was alone in life. From the Scripture text we get the hint that he was no longer a young man. The years were passing by.

And then, out of nowhere comes the right woman for him. He apparently didn't expect romance to strike. Yet God blessed him with a beautiful, godly wife. In time, he became the father of a son as well—which, for a Jewish man, was one of life's most wanted blessings. God came through for Boaz in the end.

Finally, look at the foreign girl, Ruth. She was an early widow, which no doubt broke her heart. She followed her mother-in-law to a strange country, where she began with nothing. Everybody looked at her strangely. She had to go out into a farmer's field and pick up scraps. She was viewed as nothing but a poor immigrant.

If you had seen her trudging slowly along the road at the end of a hot, exhausting day in the field, you might have said, like observers sometimes say today, "Where's the blessing of God? Obviously, something's wrong here. She must not have very much faith...." But you would have been so wrong in your judgment.

I know what it is like for immigrants to try to get a toehold in a new place, because I see it all the time in our church in New York City. I watch them struggle to get their green cards so they can work legally. They come from the islands of the Caribbean, from Central America, from Africa, the Middle East, and Asia. One such newcomer is Kumiko Nakamura, who came alone in 1998 from her home in Tokyo, Japan, to attend fashion school. The only trouble was, her English was not strong enough to enter the program, so she was forced to spend a year at a small community college instead, taking ESL (English as a Second Language) and other liberal arts courses.

There Kumiko met a woman named Karen, who befriended her. Karen and her husband loved the music of our choir, so they brought this petite, young Japanese acquaintance to a Sunday afternoon service. "I was really surprised when I entered the building," Kumiko says now in her quiet voice. "Such a big place! It was quite a contrast to the Buddhist temple I had always gone to with my family back home."

Kumiko was curious enough to come back by herself. She felt something had always been lacking in her life, although she didn't know what to call it. Maybe this church could help solve the mystery for her.

She eventually made it through fashion school, graduating in 2004. "But then, I couldn't find a job," she tells. "No one needed me. I lived with a roommate in a small apartment, and I filled in with restaurant work as a hostess three nights a week, just to pay the bills. I was poor. This went on for months and months."

Discouraged, Kumiko began coming to church more regularly, since she had a lot of time on her hands. Karen gave her a Bible, and she read it—first the New Testament, then the Old Testament, and then back to the New again. She enrolled in one of our Bible classes to try to understand more.

One morning in early 2005, something strange happened. As Kumiko tells it, "I woke up at home—and it seemed there was someone in my bed, holding me closely. That whole side of the bed was warm. It was very real; it was not a dream.

"I opened my eyes to look around—and no one was there. But I knew I was being loved and cared for. I felt like I was in the arms of someone."

Kumiko was mystified by this experience and told a few friends about it. They said, "You're going crazy. You're just depressed because you can't find a job. Now you're having delusions."

She decided to clam up about the experience. But the more she puzzled over the event, the more she came to think that Jesus had come to visit her, showing how much he loved her. "It was a big thing for me," Kumiko says today, as tears fill her eyes. "I had never received that kind of love."

Kumiko registered at the church to be baptized on a Wednesday night, April 6, 2005. Ever the careful planner, she laid out her necessary change of clothes the day before. She was excited to take this public step.

But on Tuesday morning, the phone rang. A clothing design company to which she had sent her résumé many months before was now calling. "We're looking for an assistant here," the voice said. "Would you like to come for an interview tomorrow?"

"Oh, yes!" she replied as her heart leaped. "But I have an appointment at 6 p.m. It's very important."

"That's fine; we won't take long. Just come here at two o'clock."

She showed up for the interview. Things went well. At the end, the personnel director said, "Okay, would you like to try this job for a couple of hours?"

"When?" Kumiko asked.

"Right now!"

Kumiko looked at her watch and quickly calculated the available time. Yes, she could spend two more hours there and still get to the baptism by six o'clock. She plunged into the work, did the best she could, and then ran for the subway to get to the church. That night she took her stand as a declared Christian.

On Thursday morning, the phone rang again. "We'd like to hire you!" Kumiko wept with joy. Her long nightmare of job-hunting was over at last. God seemed to be taking care of her needs after all.

By the next year, Kumiko was involved in our hospitality ministry, helping visitors and ministry guests feel at home. She also joined a small group of women who share their spiritual walk with Christ. "These are my sisters," she says, "even closer than my natural sister back in Japan. I feel I belong here."

The whole idea of telling her parents about her newfound faith in Christ has been scary for Kumiko. With characteristic Asian respect for family tradition, she did not want them to feel disappointed in her. Nearly two years

> Kumiko's friends told her, "You're going crazy. You're just depressed because you can't find a job. Now you're having delusions."

passed before the day came when she happened to be sick and her mother called from Tokyo. The mother said, "I will pray for you," which led to a discussion about the God to whom Kumiko now prays. Her mother was not happy with this news.

"Even so, I feel much better now that the facts are out in the open," Kumiko says. "I don't have to hide anything from them now. I can tell anybody." Subsequent phone calls with her mother have been generally pleasant, "but I can tell she doesn't want to talk about it any further. She stays on other subjects."

Meanwhile, Kumiko's career shows the ongoing blessing of God. Her employer has indicated that soon she will have her own name brand of women's clothing accessories. She's obviously excited about that.

"I'm a different person now," she says with a smile. "I am happier. I feel free now. And I'm loved. I want to go on a mission trip someday, to be used by God to help people. I don't yet know in what way, but God will show me."

Kumiko's story illustrates for us that God keeps track of those who honor him. And he will have the last word, as he had in the case of Ruth in the Bible. Ruth's hard times and sorrow and tears gave way to smiles and laughter and rejoicing. Ruth was destined to be much more than just a Moabite housewife. She became the great-grandmother of King David!

A Fork in the Road

How did all this happen to Ruth? Was there a key moment along the way? A decisive fork in the road that changed everything? Yes, indeed. It was that day on the outskirts of town, right after her sister-in-law Orpah was persuaded to turn back and Naomi encouraged Ruth to turn back as well. That was the point at which Ruth makes a bold statement:

"Don't urge me to leave you or to turn back from you. Where you go I will go, and where you stay I will stay. Your people will be my people and your God my God. Where you die I will die, and there I will be buried. May the LORD deal with me, be it ever so severely, if even death separates you and me" (Ruth 1:16–17).

I consider this is one of the greatest verses in the Old Testament. Ruth declares that she no longer categorizes herself by her nationality or her culture. Instead, she belongs to God. God's people, as far as she is concerned, are her people. There is no turning back.

Oh, how that would help a lot of us today! If we could get it through our minds who our people *really* are, it would make such a difference. I sometimes say to my congregation in Brooklyn, "You're not Jamaican, you're not Trinidadian—you belong to *God*. It doesn't matter if you're Puerto Rican any more than it matters that I'm Ukrainian and Polish—those are just biological details. We are part of *God's* family. I don't care where you're from; if you belong to Christ, you are my brother and sister, and I'm yours."

> Ruth declared that she would no longer categorize herself by her nationality or her culture. Instead, she belonged to God.

Those verses from the book of Ruth are sometimes quoted in wedding ceremonies to evoke the commitment of the bride to the groom, and vice versa. That's fine, although a bit astray from the original context. I would like to suggest that the most bedrock application of this statement for us today is its radical commitment to God and his people. Wherever God leads us, we pledge to go. This is our identity for the rest of our lives. Ethnic background, social class, language grouping—they all mean little compared to the fact that we are bonded to Christ and his body, the church.

This is what releases the potential for future blessing, as it did for Ruth. Did you know that her name even shows up in the New Testament? On the very first page, Matthew records "the genealogy of Jesus the Messiah"—all the men in the list, that is. Almost no women get included. But when we come to verse 5, it's as if the writer can't quite help himself; he has to say, "Boaz the father of Obed, *whose mother was Ruth.*"

Matthew sneaks in a woman's name—and a Gentile immigrant woman at that! To the traditional Jewish mind, she may not have been "one of us," but God said, "She's one of *mine.* And I want her name listed in the official family tree of my Son."

Whatever hard experiences invade our lives, whenever we come to that crucial fork in the road, we must keep insisting along with Ruth that God is our God, and his people are our people. And we must keep attending to the little things, doing what's right even if it's unpopular, even if it leaves us exhausted at the end of the day. God takes note of these things. He watches the single mother who faithfully cares for her children by day and prays over them at night. He watches the businessperson who treats the customer fairly even if it costs a little more. He notices those who are faithful to God's house in spite of what's on television or at the multiplex that weekend.

God's plans for his people are not to be compared with the passing rewards of this world. What he has in mind for those who love him wholeheartedly is more than you'd ever dream. God has made you for more.

CHAPTER 12

SUPERNATURAL PEACE

Nearly everyone remembers the famous photo from V-J Day at the end of World War II, where an exuberant sailor in the middle of Times Square is kissing a nurse, whose back is bent almost horizontal. You can even buy posters of that picture today on the Internet. Alfred Eisenstaedt, the famous photographer, wrote later that he had spotted the guy

> running along the street grabbing any and every girl in sight. Whether she was a grandmother, stout, thin, old, didn't make any difference. I was running ahead of him with my Leica [camera] looking back over my shoulder.... Then suddenly, in a flash, I saw something white being grabbed. I turned around and clicked the moment the sailor kissed the nurse. People tell me that when I am in heaven they will remember this picture.[1]

Some two million people jammed the intersection that day—August 14, 1945—to uncork their joy and relief after six years of deadly conflict. No more anxious wives wondering if their husbands far away would be shot or captured ... no more children crying for Daddy in the night ... no more

191

mothers fearing a chaplain's knock at the front door. People could finally take a deep breath and look to the future without apprehension.

When war finally ceases and peace reigns at last, human emotions are overwhelming. People laugh, they cry, they shout, they run to hug their loved ones (or even strangers), they celebrate with wild abandon. No more fighting! No more casualties! No more uncertainty!

I wonder what the joyful outburst was like back in Israel when Othniel, the first judge, prevailed against the enemy so that "the land had peace for forty years" (Judg. 3:11). Then Ehud, the second judge, beat back the Moabites, "and the land had peace for eighty years" (Judg. 3:30). Deborah and Barak's campaign brought yet another forty-year period of tranquility (see Judg. 5:31). Did they dance and throw a party? Did they slap each other on the back? Did they pump the air with their fists? We know for sure that they sang. The lyrics of their victory song take up a whole page of the Bible (Judg. 5). Catch the enthusiasm in "Hear this, you kings! Listen, you rulers! I, even I, will sing to the LORD; I will praise the LORD, the God of Israel, in song" (v. 3).

Gideon showed his deepest yearnings when, while still under the grinding oppression of the Midianites, he named his little altar *Jehovah-Shalom*, which means "The LORD Is Peace" (Judg. 6:24). God used him to bring about still another forty years without conflict (Judg. 8:28).

It must have been during one of these peaceful periods that the two vulnerable women, Naomi and Ruth, made their trek safely over the roads from Moab to Bethlehem. They could travel, unescorted, without fear.

What did peace mean to the ordinary Israelite in these times? It meant children could go out and play freely, without worry of being kidnapped. It meant parents could sleep soundly at night. A farmer could work hard and know that his crops would not be confiscated; he could use his earnings to take care of his family rather than be driven into poverty.

Here in the twenty-first century, in the middle of a "war on terrorism," we long for that moment of relief, don't we? And we fear it will never come. Peace is in short supply these days.

On a more personal level, many people today yearn for peace in their own lives. Even if the nations of the world were at rest and no insurgent groups were plotting mayhem in the shadows, many individuals would still be on edge because of fighting with their spouse or their children. Stress on the interpersonal level takes a heavy toll on millions. You can be making a six-figure salary but still lie awake at night torn apart by fractured relationships. Nothing can be enjoyed—not good food, a well-played concert, an exciting sports event at the stadium, the birth of a new baby in your family. It all goes for naught without inner tranquility.

> You can be making a six-figure salary but still lie awake at night worrying about your relationships.

I grew up in the home of an alcoholic father. If my dad was drinking, there was no peace, even at two or three o'clock in the morning. Whereas most people normally feel a sense of relief when they arrive home after a hectic day—"Oh, it's good to be home again"—I felt the opposite. My relief came whenever I *left* the house. (That's part of the reason I spent so much time playing basketball in the neighborhood. I wasn't what today is called a "gym rat," but I was a "playground rat," staying outdoors as long as I could. I would keep playing even under the lights there at Public School 92, so I wouldn't have to go home to the turmoil again.)

What a relief it was in our family when Dad finally, at the age of seventy-one, surrendered his problem to the Lord. His personal war with the bottle stopped, and we all felt the calm come over us.

The Peace of God

The words of the ancient blessing from Aaron and his priestly descendants struck a chord in the hearts of judges like Deborah and Gideon, and they still do in our hearts today:

> "The LORD bless you
> and keep you;
> the LORD make his face shine on you
> and be gracious to you;
> the LORD turn his face toward you
> and give you peace" (Num. 6:24–26).

Notice the phrasing here. This kind of peace is not just a human achievement. It is a gift from above.

That is certainly what Jesus said to his disciples during the Last Supper: "Peace I leave with you; *my peace* I give you. I do not give to you as the world gives. Do not let your hearts be troubled and do not be afraid" (John 14:27).

What is this that the Son of God termed "my" peace? It was supernatural. This was the peace that kept him in control of himself while standing on trial before hostile and unfair authorities. This peace sustained him as he stumbled toward Golgotha. The crowd howled out their disdain for him. The soldiers then nailed him to the instrument of torture. Still, he held onto *his* peace.

The apostle Paul wrote to the Philippians a wonderful promise of God. After describing certain steps we all can take, he said in response that *"the peace of God*, which transcends all understanding, will guard your hearts and your minds in Christ Jesus" (Phil. 4:7).

This is a different thing from what the Bible calls "peace *with* God"—which, incidentally, was the title of Billy Graham's trademark book, still in print after more than fifty years. He was writing about the great benefit of salvation. As Romans 5:1 puts it, "Therefore, since we have been justified through faith, we have peace with God through our Lord Jesus Christ." The wrath of God is no longer hanging over our heads. We have confessed our sins to God. He has forgiven us because of the sacrifice of Jesus, and we have been accepted into his family. He has granted us pardon, so that our offenses have been cleared, and now we are in a state of *peace with God*. This is indeed a wonderful blessing.

> The peace of God is far more than just "having a good day."

But the peace *of* God, on the other hand, goes beyond our mental comprehension. It is a state of living that should characterize the rest of our years on earth—and beyond, into eternity. It's far more than just "having a good day." You could be living in a hut somewhere in the middle of a terrible drought ... and still be the happiest person on the planet, because you possess the peace of God. This is deeper than just having adequate food and shelter, let alone a new car. This is *shalom*—that wonderful Hebrew word that means completeness, wholeness, blessing for the total person.

Peace is not just the absence of frustration, anxiety, or turbulence. It is life the way God designed it to be. It is a piece of heaven, the place of no tears, the place where *shalom* rules. We can hardly imagine it.

God wants us to enjoy this kind of blessing here on earth. He has promised us *his peace*. We frequently ask him to give us other things—more money, for example, or a promotion at work, or a healing of some kind. All kinds of people say to us ministers, "Would you pray that God would work a miracle in my life?"

"What kind of miracle?" we respond.

"Well, I really need a better job" (or a turnaround in a child's behavior, or some other request).

Rarely do we ever hear, "Pastor, please lay hands on me and pray for God to visit me with his supernatural peace."

Peace is not just getting a raise, finding a more attractive boyfriend or girlfriend, or going on vacation to the south of France. It is that deep sense that God is in charge of my life, and he is working out the best for me, whether I understand it at the moment or not. He is saying, "I want to be with you at all times because I love you. No matter where you are and what is going wrong in your circumstances, I will lead you in the path of my peace."

The trouble is, someone else is working 24/7 to cheat us out of this supernatural peace. That someone is Satan. Anything that God treasures for his people, the devil tries to rip off. He especially likes to rob our hearts of peace.

How true is the proverb that says, "A heart at peace gives life to the body, but envy rots the bones" (14:30). Medical science keeps discovering in these years what the Bible has known all along—that stress and discord are not good for your physiology. All kinds of studies keep coming out to document how the white blood cells and other physical components are at risk when we're churned up in our spirit.

Sports psychologists are exploring the mind-body connection as well. They tell golfers that after hitting a bad shot, they have to take a deep breath and clear their mind of all negativity. If they don't, the next shot is most likely going to veer off into the woods, too.

Our whole life can be thrown out of balance by the lack

of "a heart at peace." That, of course, is exactly what the devil wants. He pursues his evil goals in four ways: he makes accusations, stirs up animosity, floods us with anxiety, and pollutes our minds with garbage. But with God's help, we can reclaim peace. Here's how:

1. Resist Accusations

Satan loves bringing up the past, reminding us of things we can't change now. *I know what you did ten years ago*, he whispers. *Remember how you cheated your employer and got away with it? But God saw it, don't you know? Do you think he just forgets that kind of stuff? How do you think you're going to enjoy the blessing of God today with all that in your background?*

One of Satan's names in the Bible is "the accuser of our brothers and sisters" (Rev. 12:10). That verse goes on to declare, "[he] accuses them before our God day and night." He loves to spite God, saying things like, *See how I take your peace away from your people? They can't hold onto it when I come around and remind them of all the rotten things they've done.*

> Satan loves bringing up the past, reminding us of things we can't change now. *I know what you did ten years ago*, he whispers.

Yes, we can! By resisting the accusation we can hold on to God's peace. In Philippians 4, the apostle Paul promises that "the peace of God" also gives us a way to defend ourselves. In verse 4 he encourages us to "rejoice in the Lord always. I will say it again: Rejoice!" When we lift up our hearts to the Lord and rejoice in what he has done for us, we neutralize the accusations. We look toward the fact that we are on our way to heaven. We are going there for sure—and the devil is not! He's headed for the opposite place to be punished forever.

Meanwhile, we are on track to the glories of the celestial city.

It doesn't do any good to start reasoning with Satan. Some people say to him, "Yes, that was pretty bad what I did, wasn't it? I'm really going to do better now. I hope my good deeds will outweigh my bad deeds in the end." This is a sure way to lose your peace in about thirty seconds. Your spiritual life will be up and down like a yo-yo. The fact is, if you have confessed your sins to God and received his forgiveness, *there's no longer any record of them in heaven*. God is saying, "What sins? I'm looking at the ledger here, and I don't see any transgressions at all." The blood of Christ has cleansed you of all unrighteousness (1 John 1:9).

That's a pretty good reason to rejoice in the Lord!

Carol and I know a dear woman who has walked with Christ for many years. Before knowing the Lord, she had four children by three different fathers. The kids are all grown now, but the enemy regularly nags her about her past conduct. She came to us in tears one day. "I don't know ... I'm just remembering the kind of life I led," she said. "What was I thinking, hopping in bed with all those different men? I keep hearing this voice in my head—*You lived like an animal....*" At this, she turned her face away in shame.

That is the voice of the accuser. We counseled this woman to resist the accusation, to stand instead on the fact that her past has been wiped clean. She has a new beginning in Christ. The price he paid on the cross was "to present you holy in his sight, without blemish and free from accusation" (Col. 1:22). When we rejoice in this awesome provision for our sins, we can hang onto our peace. In fact, we are able to be a living example of what Paul wrote at the end of his letter to the Romans: "The God of peace will soon crush Satan under your feet" (Rom. 16:20). What a marvelous triumph this produces in us!

2. Resolve Animosity

In addition to making accusations, Satan robs us of peace by stirring up bad feelings toward another person. Someone abuses us emotionally or verbally, and we start nursing a grudge. We brood about the offense: *I can't believe she just walked out on me ... I can't believe he didn't say hello when we passed one another in the hall ... I married into this family, and they treat me like dirt, even though they think my husband [or wife] walks on water ... I worked really hard on that solo, but they gave the part to somebody else....* This kind of animosity is sure to drain our peace.

Philippians 4 describes two women in the church who were out of sorts with each other. The apostle Paul even put their two names right out in the open for everyone to read: "I plead with Euodia and I plead with Syntyche to be of the same mind in the Lord. Yes, and I ask you, my true companion, help these women ..." (vv. 2–3). If you got your name in the Bible only one time, wouldn't you hate to have it show up under these conditions? What if an apostle wrote, "I plead with Pastor Jim Cymbala and Pastor Charles Hammond [one of our longtime associates here in Brooklyn] to get along in the Lord"? We both would be very embarrassed.

Notice that these women were not two novices who had just become Christians the week before. They had done many good things for the Lord. Paul said they had "contended at my side in the cause of the gospel" (v. 3). They were up there in the same league with Priscilla and Phoebe and other women of the first century who carried out important work for God. Yet here they were, having a fight. It was public enough that the apostle went ahead and brought the issue out before the whole Philippian church.

And he did not say, as we are prone to say in our day, "Well, that's too bad, isn't it? But it's not my business. Let them work it out on their own."

No, Paul wrote to an unnamed person he called simply "my true companion" (v. 3) and said, in essence, "Jump in there and *do something!* Get those two women in a room, and say, 'Come on—we have to work this out. No more fighting and fussing. You hurt her? Or she hurt you? Well, we're not leaving this room until you two are at peace. We're going to talk and pray this through.'"

This is the ministry of peacemaking, which Jesus said was a blessed thing (Matt. 5:9). He wanted to see his peace reign in people's lives, especially those who claim to be his disciples.

> What good is an offering or a praise song or a fancy prayer if you're mad at somebody? What is God more interested in, a song or reconciliation?

A few verses later, Jesus urges that we take the initiative ourselves when we are crosswise of someone: "If you are offering your gift at the altar and there remember that your brother or sister has something against you, leave your gift there in front of the altar. First go and be reconciled to that person; then come and offer your gift" (Matt. 5:23–24). Restoring peace and resolving animosity is more important than carrying on a worship service, Jesus said. After all, what good is an offering or a praise song or a fancy prayer if you're mad at somebody? How can you honestly sing "We Worship and Adore You" if the "we" includes somebody you despise, or somebody who despises you? What is God more interested in, a song or reconciliation that leads to peace?

Sometimes we say, "Oh, I couldn't go to anybody like

that. I'm just not the type." Well, then, we're an unbiblical type. God wants us to get peace back in our relationships so we can then worship him with open and sincere hearts.

What if you try to approach the other person, and they tell you to get lost? Then you can arrive at peace through a different route. You can hand this situation over to God, knowing you have done what he asked you to do. This is why the Bible says, "If it is possible, as far as it depends on you, live at peace with everyone" (Rom. 12:18). Granted, sometimes the other person's heart is so hard that peace is not possible. But we must do everything within our power to bring about reconciliation. If the person lives in another state now, we can pick up the phone and call them. Our job is to have the right spirit, to be honest, to apologize even if we think we might be misunderstood—and then leave the results to God.

3. Release Anxiety

Another tactic Satan uses to steal our peace is to flood us with *anxiety*. We all know the things that keep us awake at night: the future ... our mounting bills ... our wayward son or daughter ... the health issue our doctor hasn't yet figured out ... safety in our neighborhood. When we are obsessed with these things, we don't sleep well, and we don't rest in God's love.

Philippians 4 has a remedy for this, too. It says, "Do not be anxious about anything, but in every situation, by prayer and petition, with thanksgiving, present your requests to God" (v. 6).

We take the weight that is bearing down on us and give it to God in prayer. There is an actual transfer here; we lift the weight up and off from our backs, and he takes it for handling. The thing that has been too heavy for us is a light weight in his hands. We come like a little child. We don't try to formulate a prayer that sounds like the King James Version. We say instead, "Father, I'm really bothered by this. I'm worried about how it's going to turn out. Would you take care of it for me? How about if I just unload this onto you? You're so much stronger than I am."

The result, if we truly leave our anxieties to God, is supernatural peace.

We often recite our problems to God, but there's no real transfer. The minute we say "amen," we feel just as weighed down as when we started. Our minds are still consumed with "What in the world am I going to do about this?" Nothing was, in fact, handed over to the Almighty One.

E. Stanley Jones, the great Methodist missionary to India, wrote a one-page devotional in the early 1940s with a shocking title: "Worry Is Atheism." Many churchgoing people would claim to believe in God even though they still worry "once in a while." What did this man of God mean? He wrote:

> A person who worries says, "I cannot trust God; I'll take things into my own hands. Result? Worry, frustration, incapacity to meet the dreaded thing when it does come.... Worry says, "God doesn't care, and so He won't do anything—I'll have to worry it through." Faith says, "God does care, and He and I will work it out together. I'll supply the willingness, and He will supply the power—with that combination we can do anything."[2]

When we truly release our anxieties to God, "the peace of God, which transcends all understanding, will guard your hearts and your minds in Christ Jesus" (Phil. 4:7). That is a divine guarantee! The imagery here is military; the peace of God is portrayed as a sentry, marching in crisp cadence around and around your *heart* (the deepest part of your emotions) as well as your *mind* (the center of your thought life). *Hut-two-three-four, hut-two-three-four* ... the divine sentry keeps circling you hour after hour, making sure nothing harmful gets through to touch either your emotions or your conscious thoughts. You are fully protected.

I saw this level of peace not long ago at the graveside of our associate pastor Carlo Boekstaaf, whom I mentioned earlier. I stood there holding the hand of Ingrid, his wonderful and godly wife, who was now left alone much sooner than she had expected. As the officiating minister that day, I fought to control my emotions, because Carlo was one of my closest friends.

Ingrid sensed what I was going through, and she quietly murmured as we stood there, "Don't worry, Pastor. It will be fine. I'm going to be all right. And you will, too."

I thought to myself, *My goodness—I'm the minister here, and she's the widow. I'm supposed to be saying those things to her!* Her peace was not logical. It was absolutely supernatural—the kind that can only be called "the peace of God."

Anxiety is the natural enemy of peace. But it can be erased as we release our anxieties, cares and worries upon the Lord.

4. Renew Your Mental "Atmosphere"

The fourth arena that needs our attention is the *atmosphere* that surrounds us, capturing our mental state. The devil loves to fill our minds with garbage. Through what we see and hear in the media, through the books we read and the people we meet, through all the noise of daily life in our culture, he seeks to contaminate our thinking until we truly cannot think straight. The nonstop flood of images and ideas and sounds coming our way through everything from huge movie screens to tiny earphones can destroy our peace if we let it.

Philippians 4:8–9 boldly advises, "Finally, brothers and sisters, whatever is true, whatever is noble, whatever is right, whatever is pure, whatever is lovely, whatever is admirable—if anything is excellent or praiseworthy—*think about such things* ... and the God of peace will be with you."

Whatever is true ... we need to live in reality. The fantasy world, from romantic novels to video games, doesn't exist. The more we try to hide in those daydreams, the more unsettled we will be when the lights turn off and we have to return to the real world.

Whatever is noble ... the word means "worthy of respect." God doesn't want us wallowing in things that are cheap, vulgar, or low-class. They rob us of his peace.

Whatever is right ... yes, there is still a category called "right" in this world, and a category called "wrong." Many people like to imagine that such terms are outdated, and everything is now relative. That's not true.

Whatever is pure ... in other words, the opposite of dirty, lustful, tainted, and off-color. God doesn't want these things in our minds. They pollute our thought life and rob us of his peace.

Whatever is lovely ... the opposite of ugly and grotesque. Why pay money for things, from DVDs to artwork to clothing, that are patently nasty? Such things are bound to have an effect on our thoughts.

Whatever is admirable ... we all need role models to look up to. Too often in the world of entertainment and sports and even politics, we see anti-heroes—the kind of man or woman you *don't* want your child to emulate. Paul the apostle says to keep looking until you find those whom you can admire.

If anything is excellent or praiseworthy ... in other words, don't settle for the mediocre. Don't put up with things that are "just okay." Reach for things that set a high standard.

When we think on these things, it makes a huge difference in our mental atmosphere. We inhabit a world that is orderly and peaceful. We focus our attention on the good elements of life instead of the sleazy.

Not long ago a young woman came to me at the end of our morning service to say she was struggling as a young Christian. She was a single mom with a ten-year-old son. "Something's wrong," she confessed. "I'm just not doing very well."

> God doesn't want us wallowing in things that are cheap, vulgar or low-class. They rob us of his peace.

I asked a few questions, trying to get to the bottom of her malaise. "Why do you think you're not experiencing God's peace?" I asked. "Tell me what you think might be at the root of that."

"Well, you know," she answered, "back when I was eighteen years old, somebody cast a spell on me...."

"Oh, really?"

"Yes, and then when I was twenty-three or twenty-four, I was dating this guy. But somebody didn't like it that I was seeing him, and so they put another spell on me...."

Things started to click in my brain. "And that's what you're thinking about this much later?" I said.

"Yes, I guess so," she admitted.

"No wonder you don't have the peace of God," I replied. "Look, when you belong to Jesus, there is no witchcraft that will work on you. You're his property now. He doesn't tolerate outside spirits messing with his child. Instead of thinking about the occult, I want you to think about the good promises of God. Let me see the Bible you're reading...."

I discovered she had a fairly hard-to-understand translation, so I got her one she could understand more easily. I also picked out a spiritual book I thought would help her. She needed to think about true things, noble things, right things, instead of the lies of the devil. Only then would she be able to live in a state of peace.

We need to recognize the instant a thought enters our mental atmosphere that is going to pollute us. We need to tell Satan to take his garbage and get out. The prophet Isaiah had it exactly right when he wrote, "You [God] will keep in perfect peace those whose minds are steadfast, because they trust in you" (Isa. 26:3).

Personal peace is a quality of the Promised Land that God is bringing us into. It is part of the greater blessing he intends for our lives. He cannot stand the thought of us succumbing to accusations, animosities, anxieties, and a bad mental atmosphere. He is calling us to something higher—a life infused with the supernatural peace of God. We must arise and receive this wonderful provision from his hand.

CHAPTER 13

A WORD
TO REMEMBER

Promises can be tricky things. If you make them, you have to keep them. More than a few political candidates have said things out on the campaign trail that they couldn't seem to deliver after they won the election. The legislature or the bureaucracy or the courts wouldn't go along with their idea, and the promise went unfulfilled. Voters don't appreciate that.

All of us who are parents know that children take promises very, very seriously. If you say to an eight-year-old, "Sure, we'll go to the park tonight after dinner," you had better not forget. The same eight-year-old, of course, may frequently forget to make his bed, feed the dog, or bring his bike in from the rain. But he has a photographic memory when it comes to *your* commitments to him. Any shortcoming on your part is sure to bring on a storm of protest: "But you *promised!*"

God, by contrast, is an entirely reliable promise maker. The reason Joshua could march into Canaan with confidence is because God had promised it to him. The reason Joshua's army could fight with courage is because God had said, "I will be with you" (Josh. 1:5). In the time of the judges, when things got really crazy, someone remembered God's promise about prayer, so they "cried out to the LORD" more than once (Judg. 3:9; 3:15; 6:6; 10:10).

In fact, God seems to enjoy making promises. Time and again he announces in advance what he's going to do. Before Abram ever left Ur of the Chaldeans, God promised, "I will make you into a great nation, and I will bless you" (Gen. 12:2). Once Abram got to Canaan and started looking around, God told him repeatedly, "All the land that you see I will give to you and your offspring forever" (Gen. 13:15 and elsewhere).

Before Jacob ever left his uncle's employment in Paddan Aram, God said to him, "Go back to your country and your relatives, and I will make you prosper" (Gen. 32:9) — even though his brother Esau was poised to avenge the trick Jacob had played on him long ago.

Before Joseph was lifted to prominence and leadership in the nation of Egypt, God already gave him two dreams that predicted this (Gen. 37:5–9).

Before Moses ever ventured back from the desert where he had hidden for forty years, God promised him at the burning bush, "Now go; I will help you speak and will teach you what to say" (Exod. 4:12).

While David was still a young nobody out in the field, God's prophet was sent to anoint him as the future king (1 Sam. 16:1–13).

Before Jesus came the first time, there were myriad promises about where he would be born, what he would do, how he would be received, and how he would die.

Before he left to return to heaven, he promised the eleven disciples that "in a few days you will be baptized with the Holy Spirit, ... [and] you will receive power" (Acts 1:5, 8).

Why does God do this kind of thing? Why does he so often "tip his hand" ahead of time?

I can think of at least two reasons. First, *God secures the glory this way*. Nobody can say, "Wasn't that an interesting coincidence how that happened?" The script was already published in advance through the promise of God. We have no choice but to give him honor and praise as a result.

Second, *God wants to teach us to trust him*. He sometimes informs those who belong to him about what he is going to do, and we must trust his word, even though it seems unlikely if not impossible. Sometimes he delays a long time. Abraham and his wife had to wait forever, it seemed to them, for the promise of an heir to come true. They were getting older and older. Would God actually make good on his promise after so long? It was a matter of trust.

No one should say, as we sometimes cynically say about people whom we know all too well, "Ah, promises, promises...." This is *God* talking to us! He keeps his word. It is part of his character. He would not be God if he didn't.

Remember the Word

If we are ever fearful that God might not follow through on his promises, there is a two-line verse in Psalm 119—yes, the longest chapter in the Bible—that fits this situation. I am aware that many Christians skip over this psalm because it is so long (176 verses) and seemingly repetitive. If you're getting ready for bed in the late evening and just want to read one psalm before you turn out the light, don't pick this one—you will still be reading at four in the morning.

Psalm 119 is actually an elaborate acrostic built on the twenty-two letters of the Hebrew alphabet, with eight verses for each letter (22 x 8 = 176). The beginning for the letter *zayin* (comparable to our English letter Z) comes in verse 49 and is a powerful statement for anyone to whom God has made a promise. It is a prayer of reinforcement:

> Remember your word to your servant,
>   for you have given me hope.

We should put this verse onto posters and hang them on our walls. We should engrave it on plaques and mirrors. We should design it into needlework patterns. We should, at the very least, emblazon it into our memory banks so it can become a spiritual anchor in our prayer times.

What is this "word" that the psalmist holds up for our attention? Basically, it is the Bible. Here is where we find God's irrevocable promises about many things. The Bible is the foundation for all doctrine and matters of faith. Because of that, we can call on God and say, "Remember what you promised in your Word to your people. Follow through, O Lord!"

It sounds almost audacious to remind God of anything, doesn't it? He is omniscient, after all. But this is not being impolite toward God. If anything, this is affirming his character. He welcomes the Psalm 119:49 kind of praying. As Charles Spurgeon, the great British preacher of the late 1800s, once said, "Whether we like it or not, asking is the rule of the kingdom."[1]

The Brooklyn Tabernacle Choir sings a song by Luther Barnes that never fails to lift my spirit and cause me to stand with affirmation.

> Everything he said in his Word
> He will do it for you.
> Every prophecy he gave, every promise he made
> He will do it for you.

If you only trust him and let him have his way,
He'll work things out for you.
Only believe, and you will see
He will do it for you.

He will do it, he will do it,
He will do it, he will do it....
My God will do it for you.[2]

A Personalized Word

In addition to remembering God's Word, it's important to listen for the specific things God might say to us. God often takes the general promises in his written Word and applies them to our lives in a personal way. The psalmist hints at this by talking about "your word *to your servant*." There seems to be a special application here. This is what you and I experience when we may be reading the Bible and a particular verse almost jumps off the page in front of us. We may be praying, quietly waiting before the Lord, and an unexpected thought or possibility stirs our hearts. We may be singing in church or listening to a sermon, and we sense in our spirits that God is speaking a personalized word just to us.

It may be something he wants us to do for him.

It may be the answer to a problem that has plagued us for a long time.

It may be an assurance that things are going to work out all right after all, whether in our family, our career, our church, or some other arena.

Paul wrote to Timothy about his ordination, when something specific "was given you through prophecy when the body of elders laid their hands on you" (1 Tim. 4:14). These were not words for the congregation in general; they were meant for Timothy alone.

God has a way of planting things in our hearts at odd times and in odd places. He can even take us by surprise. But if we make ourselves open to his voice, whether in our devotional practice or in the middle of busy traffic on the way home from work, he can invade our lives and reveal his purposes for us.

This kind of word especially can become an anchor to our prayer times. Let this be the cry of every Christian, like a persistent child: "O God, don't forget your word to your servant! It's the bedrock of my hope. It's what I cling to. It's what keeps me from drowning in the waters of despair. Remember what you said, Lord! Keep it right there in front of your eyes."

God has said in his Word, "I am the LORD; those who hope in me will not be disappointed" (Isa. 49:23). Romans 10:11 quotes another verse from Isaiah with this wording: "Anyone who believes in him will never be put to shame." These are rock-solid promises to which we must cling. We can pray, "God, at one time in the past you spoke something to me. You caused me to anticipate something from you in my life. It has not happened yet. But that word is still alive in my heart. Are you the kind of God who would speak something to me and then let me down? No! That isn't your nature.

"So I cling to your word with anticipation. Don't disappoint me, God. Remember what you said to me. I know you will come through. I fully expect your promise to hold true!"

Jesus once came to a good friend of his who was going through a terrible time—the death of her brother—and said, "Your brother will rise again" (John 11:23). Martha could not entirely absorb that promise. When she and the others led Jesus out to the burial cave an hour or so later and he suggested removing the stone, she protested that the smell of decay would be pungent by now.

"Then Jesus said, 'Did I not tell you that if you believe, you will see the glory of God?'" (John 11:40)

Remember the word! Don't give up on it! God never backs away from one of his promises, and we shouldn't either. Cling to it in faith and expectation. Underline Psalm 119:49 in your Bible. Turn to it often. Lift it up before God as a reinforcement of his covenant promise to you. Let it strengthen your confidence in him.

The Promise of Things to Come

My wife, Carol, still remembers the day back in her home on Devon Road in Woodbridge, New Jersey, when, as a shy fifteen-year-old, she was making a bed. She fluffed the sheet into the air so it would land in the right position—and as she did, she suddenly saw herself raising her arms in the same motion, only now as an adult woman ... in front of a massive choir! She was directing a song, and the singers were of all different colors and races. They were enthusiastically following her guidance, moving and rejoicing before the Lord.

What in the world! She was only fifteen years old. How would such a thing ever develop for little, unknown Carol Hutchins?

The memory of that incident has helped Carol many times over the years when she felt discouraged or overwhelmed with the work of the choir. She knows God would not have shown her that picture without helping her to fulfill it. It has bolstered her tremendously.

God does not waste his communication. He is always working from the long perspective. We may forget all about what he says, but he does not. He brings to pass what he has promised. It is for us to keep believing, keep waiting, keep praying, and keep holding on.

If God has told you he's going to reclaim your wayward child, *it is going to happen.*

If God has told you he's going to provide for your financial needs, *it is going to happen.*

If God has told you he's going to put you into a field of ministry you've never tried before, and you're going to be effective regardless, *it is going to happen.*

If God has told you he's going to bring a baby into your arms, *it is going to happen.*

If God has told you he's going to break that long-standing bondage or weakness in your life, *it is going to happen.*

He may not come through as quickly as you would like. But he is never late. He operates by his own calendar. And the results are good for us in the end. I have known people whom God impressed with a dream back in childhood. It took years for the dream to come true. But God did not forget, and neither did that person. In time, the vision became reality.

What Has God Promised *You*?

Was there ever a time when you felt God spoke a word into your heart about what he would do with you or for you? Maybe it was during a quiet time alone with God. Maybe it was something that happened at the end of a church service. Hang onto that. Pin this Scripture to the front wall of your mind:

> God is not a human, that he should lie,
> not a human being, that he should change his mind.
> Does he speak and then not act?
> Does he promise and not fulfill? (Num. 23:19).

Not only does Satan want to rob you of peace, as we mentioned earlier, but he also wants to snatch away that special word that produces faith and expectation. He wants you to give up on ever seeing it happen. He will tell you you're too old now; you've missed your chance.

But the reality of walking in God's promises is that *he made you for more*. And there is no way imaginable that he will not bring to pass what he has said. You are his beloved child, and he is the best Father in the world. He will not disappoint you. He will do what he has promised in your life.

NOTES

Chapter 1: Step Up

1. "Keep on Making a Way" words and music by Percy Gray Jr.
   © 2002 Saved Children's Music administered by BMI and Slickey
   Music/BMI. Recorded on *Live ... This Is Your House* Disc 1
   © 2003 The Brooklyn Tabernacle Choir, licensed and marketed by
   M2 Communications.
2. Cited in *Footprints for Pilgrims* (1915; reprint, Sunbury, PA: Believers
   Bookshelf, 1970), 35.
3. For one explanation of this, see "The Conquest and the Ethical
   Question of War," *TNIV Study Bible* (Grand Rapids: Zondervan,
   2006), 294.
4. New King James Version.

Chapter 2: An Assignment Just for You

1. Cited in *Footprints for Pilgrims* (1915; reprint, Sunbury, PA: Believers
   Bookshelf, 1970), 41.
2. Wayne and Diane Tesch, *Unlocking the Secret World: A Unique
   Christian Ministry to Abused, Abandoned, and Neglected Children*
   (Wheaton, IL: Tyndale, 1995).
3. James H. Olthuis, *Keeping Our Troth* (San Francisco: Harper & Row,
   1986), 133–34.

Chapter 3: The Place of God's Blessing

1. New American Standard Bible.
2. George Müller, *A Narrative of Some of the Lord's Dealings with George Müller, Written by Himself* (Muskegon, Mich.: Dust and Ashes Publications, 2003), 730, italics added.
3. Cited in Horatius Bonar, *Words Old and New* (1866; reprint, Edinburgh: Banner of Truth, 1994), 21.
4. Andraé Crouch, "The Blood Will Never Lose Its Power," © 1966 Manna Music, Inc.
5. Kenneth Morris, © 1957 Martin and Morris Music, BMI.

Chapter 4: The Forgotten One

1. "Fill My Cup, Lord," © 1959 by Richard Blanchard. Assigned to Sacred Songs (A Div. of Word, Inc.).
2. His rash vow that resulted in his daughter's untimely death; see Judges 11:30–40.
3. His later craftsmanship of a golden ephod that became a national idol, thus reinstating the false worship that had gotten Israel in trouble in the first place; see Judges 8:22–27.
4. D. L. Moody, *Glad Tidings: Comprising Sermons and Prayer Meeting Talks Delivered at the N. Y. Hippodrome* (New York: E. B. Treat, 1876), 227.
5. Frank Bartleman, in one of the early editions of *The Apostolic Faith*, a newspaper published intermittently starting in 1906 by the Azusa Street Mission, Los Angeles.
6. "Our War Congress," *Christian Mission Magazine*, Sept. 1878; cited in an email from Capt. Heather Coles, Salvation Army Heritage Center, London, U.K., 2007.

Chapter 5: Lesson from the Bayou

1. All quotations in this section are from the book *Cain's Redemption* by Dennis Shere (Chicago: Northfield, 2005).
2. Cited in Horatius Bonar, *Words Old and New* (1866; reprint, Edinburgh: Banner of Truth, 1994), 21.

Chapter 6: Not So Fast!

1. Cited in Horatius Bonar, *Words Old and New* (1866; reprint, Edinburgh: Banner of Truth, 1994), 68.

Chapter 7: Wholehearted for the Long Haul

1. See, for example, http://www2.tbo.com/content/2008/feb/06/frank-buckles-americas-last-living-world-war-i-vet/. Accessed April 29, 2008.
2. New King James Version
3. Cited in Horatius Bonar, *Words Old and New* (1866; reprint, Edinburgh: Banner of Truth, 1994), 83.
4. Cited in the "Patrick Hamilton" entry by J. D. Douglas, *The New International Dictionary of the Christian Church* (Grand Rapids: Zondervan, 1978), 449.

Chapter 8: "What's Up with This?"

1. For the full account, see *Fresh Faith* (Grand Rapids: Zondervan, 1999), 121–26.
2. E. M. Bounds, *The Necessity of Prayer*, in *The Complete Works of E. M. Bounds on Prayer* (Grand Rapids: Baker, 1990), 35.
3. See chapter 4 of my book *Fresh Wind, Fresh Fire* (Grand Rapids: Zondervan, 1997), 53–66.
4. G. V. Wigram, cited in *Footprints for Pilgrims* (1915; reprint, Sunbury, PA: Believers Bookshelf, 1970), 17.

Chapter 9: The Enemy Within

1. Cited in Horatius Bonar, *Words Old and New* (1866; reprint, Edinburgh: Banner of Truth, 1994), 59.
2. This sermon constitutes a chapter in *Treasury of the World's Great Sermons*, compiled by Warren Wiersbe (Grand Rapids: Kregel, 1993), starting on page 120.
3. Andrew Murray, *Humility* (Old Tappan, NJ: Revell, 1961 edition), 15.

Chapter 10: Objection Overruled

1. Horatius Bonar, *Words Old and New* (1866; reprint, Edinburgh: Banner of Truth, 1994), 278.
2. J. H. Merle d'Aubigné, *The History of the Reformation of the Sixteenth Century*, Book 2, Chap. 1, Par. 1 (1835 ed.). www.lgmarshall.org/Daubigne/daubigne_refhistory02_01.html. Accessed April 2, 2008.

Chapter 12: Supernatural Peace

1. http://artscenecal.com/ArticlesFile/Archive/Articles1997/Articles0397/AEisenstaedt.html. Accessed April 2, 2008.
2. E. Stanley Jones, *Abundant Living* (Nashville: Abingdon, 1942), 74.

Chapter 13: A Word to Remember

1. Charles H. Spurgeon, *Spurgeon on Prayer and Spiritual Warfare* (New Kensington, PA: Whitaker House, 1998), 122.
2. "God's Promise," words and music by Luther Barnes, © 1997 International Atlanta Music, Lubar Music/BMI; recorded on CD and DVD *I'm Amazed ... LIVE*, The Brooklyn Tabernacle Choir, © 2006 The Brooklyn Tabernacle, marketed by INO Records.

THE Brooklyn
TABERNACLE
~CHOIR~

Worship with 3500 believers at The Brooklyn Tabernacle in this LIVE recording featuring their 300 voice choir as they "Say YES" to the call of Christ. From powerful worship favorites like **Holy Is The Lord** to new anthems like **We Fill The Sanctuary**, *I'll Say Yes* will bring you into a place of spirited praise and deep worship.

· Recorded LIVE at The Brooklyn Tabernacle In New York
· A Monumental Worship Experience
· Powerful, Exuberant Praise...Deep Intimate Worship
· Available in CD and DVD

DVD Includes:
· The Full Worship Concert PLUS...
· 60 Minute Docu-video About The Brooklyn Tabernacle
· Church Members' Testimonies
· Interviews with Pastors Jim and Carol Cymbala

I'LL SAY *Yes*

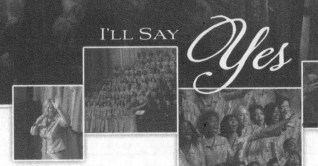

INTEGRITY
MUSIC.

Available at your Favorite Christian Bookstore
or www.integritymusic.com

Printed in the USA
CPSIA information can be obtained
at www.ICGtesting.com
LVHW051532210724
785408LV00008B/88

9 780310 340881